Unraveling the Seven Myths of Reading

Assessment and Intervention Practices for Counteracting Their Effects

Frank B. May, Ph.D.
Portland State University

Allyn and Bacon

Boston ▪ London ▪ Toronto ▪ Sydney ▪ Tokyo ▪ Singapore

To Dr. Louise Fulton, California State University at San Bernardino, in honor of her forty-year career of unraveling the myths of learning and teaching

---

Vice President: Paul A. Smith
Senior Editor: Arnis E. Burvikovs
Editorial Assistant: Patrice Mailloux
Executive Marketing Manager: Lisa Kimball
Manufacturing Buyer: Julie McNeill
Cover Administrator: Jennifer Hart
Electronic Composition: Omegatype Typography, Inc.

A Pearson Education Company
160 Gould Street
Needham Heights, MA 02494

Internet: www.abacon.com

Between the time Website information is gathered and published, some sites may have closed. Also, the transcription of URLs can result in typographical errors. The publisher would appreciate notification where these occur so that they may be corrected in subsequent editions.

Library of Congress Cataloging-in-Publication Data
May, Frank B.
Unraveling the seven myths of reading : assessment and intervention practices for counteracting their effects / Frank B. May.
p. cm.
ISBN 0-205-30914-3
1. Reading. 2. Reading comprehension. 3. Reading disability. I. Title.

LB1050.2 .M364 2001
428.4—dc21 00-044197

Printed in the United States of America
10 9 8 7 6 5 4 3 2 1 04 03 02 01 00

CONTENTS

PREFACE

The seven myths of reading are like Homer's Sirens, those attractive creatures who lured the sailors of long ago onto the rocks, destroying their ships and keeping the men as their lovers. The most beautiful siren, in my imagination, was wrapped in layer on layer of exquisite cloth. If one layer of cloth was peeled off, the next layer would be even more exquisite, the third layer even more so, until you had unraveled seven layers of cloth. When the siren was completely unclothed you found nothing inside but hot, stale air.

This treatise, textbook, and handbook is based on examination of well-designed research and theory published since 1960. It is also based on the author's own professional assessment, instructional interventions, and professional recommendations for approximately 4,000 ineffective readers over the course of four decades. Finally, it is based on the reported observations, assessments, and instructional interventions since 1966 by approximately 3,000 in-service public school teachers, all graduate students of the author.

Unraveling the Seven Myths of Reading was designed for courses, seminars, workshops, and individual educators. The intended audience is mainly that of classroom teachers, university students, literacy scholars, and professors of reading or literacy. The five interrelated areas of study include **theory, research, case studies, assessment,** and **instruction.**

The following are twelve specific courses and other uses for *Unraveling the Seven Myths of Reading:*

- **a.** The second half of a beginning course on reading instruction
- **b.** A second undergraduate or first graduate course on reading instruction
- **c.** A reading course on corrective assessment and intervention
- **d.** A master's or doctoral seminar on reading psychology and related issues
- **e.** A master's or doctoral seminar on belief systems and their effects on instructional practices
- **f.** A curriculum theory course (supplement)
- **g.** A special-education course (a supplement on reading problems)
- **h.** A required course for achieving reading specialist credentials
- **i.** A desktop handbook for K–12 teachers, aides, and tutors

- **j.** A desktop handbook for community college teachers of remedial reading
- **k.** A desktop handbook for school principals, superintendents, and other training staff

Suggestions to the Reader

This book is designed to be read for any or all of six purposes:

Purpose 1. Expanding or modifying your theoretical positions on literacy development and understanding the beliefs that impede the progress toward reading effectiveness.

Purpose 2. Viewing a summary of research reports that demonstrate the inaccuracies of each myth or belief.

Purpose 3. Examining actual case studies illustrating the problems that students and teachers may have as a result of particular myths or beliefs.

Purpose 4. Finding assessment techniques that may be used for your own self-evaluation or to determine a particular student's reading problem.

Purpose 5. Determining forms of positive intervention that may help your student or students overcome an identified reading problem.

Purpose 6. Studying in depth an individual student's reading problem (or problems).

Acknowledgments

I would like to thank the following reviewers for their helpful remarks: Judythe Patberg, University of Toledo; Amy P. Dietrich, University of Memphis; and Carol Fuhler, Iowa State University.

CHAPTER

1 The First Myth of Reading

Myth 1, Part A: We Learn to Read Mostly by Learning Words

Let's begin with a myth that doesn't want to go away. Shakespeare's Hamlet expressed it well when he responded to the innocent question of Polonius in Act 2, Scene 2:

POLONIUS: What do you read, my lord?

HAMLET: Words, words, words.

POLONIUS: What is the matter, my lord?

HAMLET: Between who?

POLONIUS: I mean, the matter that you read, my lord.

Hamlet's response of "Words, words, words" is quite similar to the attitude of a poorly taught student, Alfred by name, who has learned at an early age that he is to read in a way that satisfies adults. He has learned that adults want him to concentrate on correct pronunciation of each word that appears in a horizontal, trainlike thing called a "sentence."

To a student having trouble learning to read, this concentration on individual words can appear to lack purpose—other than getting it over with and moving on to an activity that requires strength, wit, problem-solving, or dexterity rather than this seemingly irrelevant task called "reading." An understandable feeling, wouldn't you say? How could *anyone* enjoy stumbling and mumbling over the isolated words in a sentence, while at the same time being embarrassed by the comments of his or her critical listeners.

What, Alfred? Is Reading Not at All Like Listening?

Alfred, the first case study in this chapter, was probably led astray by well-meaning adults. In his early years in school he unconsciously and unfortunately learned that reading is very different from listening. Before he arrived in school, he knew the purpose of language quite well. When he listened to an adult, for instance, he knew intuitively that he was to pay attention to the message, especially when the messenger sent it in a loud angry voice: "Shut that door, Alfred!!"

He knew intuitively that he was not expected to listen to each of those four words in a one-by-one isolated way! Instead, he had been trained through experience to purposefully concentrate on the total message, which, if followed, would keep him out of trouble. Or, in a more positive environment, he hoped that by concentrating on the total message, he would receive that fresh chocolate-chip cookie he had burst through the door to beg from his mother.

Clearly, Alfred, and all the rest of us humans, listen mainly for a purpose, and that purpose is usually to understand the message of the speaker (her promises, warnings, demands, jokes, questions, answers, directions, or descriptions). But alas, Sir Alfred, most of us adults in your life have conditioned you to *listen* for a purpose but not necessarily to *read* for a purpose. Instead, we have unwittingly conditioned you to strive for relief, relief gained by quickly "knocking off," "rubbing out," or "slaughtering" those poor little letters and words: one by one...by one...by one...by one.... The words become little soldiers of an opposing army that the reader must ***zap*** in rapid order from left to right. (If Alfred zaps them correctly, he's rewarded by a smile, or the words, "Good job!")

But, Beware, My Fellow "Good Job" Teachers

The most dangerous outcome of this overdone and insufficient feedback to such a "word-by-word reader" is the strong possibility that he will develop the wrong concept of reading, such as "reading is the hasty process of glancing at those little chains of letters and coming up with wordlike sounds" (such as RE-port instead of re-PORT; or "un-a-sal" instead of "unusual").

The "good job" teachers may be reinforcing students' erroneous concept of the reading process by praising them for getting every word "right." This can easily confirm their budding belief that reading is a process of pronouncing each word correctly. On the other hand, notice what happens when you, the wisest of all teachers, say something more honest, like this: "Okay, that time you correctly pronounced all the words in that sentence. Now let me hear what you think the author is telling you." And then, after helping your student grasp the author's meaning, you say, "Now read that same sentence as if you're the author telling me a story." And finally you praise him like this: "That was good reading, wasn't it." Your student is now involved in the process of reading for the author's meaning.

Does Alfred Have a Clue about What Reading Really Is?

By now it's probably obvious to you that Alfred's concept of what reading *really* is will become the basis for what he gains from reading, whether it's reading a story, an article, or anything else: Alfred can gain pleasure and information from actually communicating with an author, or he can gain a dislike of the reading process. It all depends on what his concept of reading is: mechanical word-reproduction or purposeful message-reproduction. (I say *reproduction,* because a reader is producing in his or her head what has been already produced in print.)

Think of this: If Alfred had been born before the invention of writing, he would have learned to speak and listen to messages (even if some were as short as one word, such as "Alfred!!"). He would not have learned to speak and listen with one isolated word after another. After writing was invented, the same would have been true: He would have learned to write and read messages, and not just words.

> Our first myth has often caused both teachers and learners to put the carriage before the horse—the word before the message. Words and messages are both important, but the goal of learning to read (both for the student and for the one helping the student) needs to be kept in perspective. It's to learn how to communicate with another human being through written messages.

Why? So the reader can gain needed information or entertainment.

How? By listening inside his or her head to the messages received from the author, by using his or her own background to understand the messages, by searching for the unwritten messages that live between the lines.

What messages? Ideas, reports, procedures, stories, directions, jokes, warnings, innuendoes, songs, critiques, and implications.

When? Whenever your student has become motivated to seek messages in writing from another human being.

Where? Wherever books, newspapers, magazines, letters, notes, computer screens, billboards, chalkboards, and cereal boxes are readily available.

Myth 1, Part B: Research Showing the Inaccuracy of the Myth, *we learn to read mostly by learning words*

> Please notice that in Part B of each chapter I will usually report only on the conclusions or the results and conclusions. As I mentioned in the preface of this book, I will be reporting only those studies or research reviews that demonstrate a high quality design. This design, of course, includes the procedures used for carrying out the study and assessing the results. Those interested in more than the results or conclusions of a particular study are advised to read the entire study in order to determine whether the procedures of the study were valid and reliable in your estimation.

It was mentioned in Part A that those who read word-by-word rather than searching for the author's message are often those who have been taught to read that way. What do some of the researchers have to say about this issue, and about the myth that we learn to read mainly by learning words?

A Longitudinal Study of a One-Dimensional Reading Strategy

Juel, C. (1988). Learning to read and write: A longitudinal study of 54 children from first through fourth grades. *Journal of Educational Psychology, 80,* 437–447.

Conclusion. Children tend to stick to the very first reading strategy they are taught to use.

Discussion. (All discussions in Part B of each chapter will be mine and not that of the author of each study.) Juel was referring primarily to the first reading strategy so often taught, namely the word-by-word phonics strategy. She discovered in her study that neophytes tend to continue this strategy until (or unless) another teacher intervenes.

It is my experience that the intervention needs to provide direct and indirect instruction on using multiple cues. Those cues include (1) spelling patterns, (2) language sounds associated with those spelling patterns, (3) syntax and morpheme cues, (4) the author's meaning of each word, (5) the reader's living experiences, and (6) the reader's memories of communications and feelings.

When phonic cues or sight vocabulary cues are emphasized more than meaningful sentences, ideas, and stories, the teacher may unintentionally keep students from acquiring the habit of combining the four major cues as they read: (1) graphophonic cues (visual letters and the sounds they represent), (2) syntax cues (the order and arrangement of words and other morphemes), (3) semantic cues (words chosen by the author), and (4) schematic cues (knowledge of the reader gained from prior experiences). When the novice reader is deprived too often of the opportunity to use those four cues simultaneously, I have found that he or she can develop the habit of reading (pseudo-reading) without searching with vigor for the meaning of the author's messages.

A Study of the One-Dimensional Strategy in Kindergartens

Durkin, D. (1988). A classroom observation study of reading instruction in kindergarten. Technical Report No. 422. Urbana, IL: Center for the Study of Reading, University of Illinois.

At the same time that Juel was publishing her study on the effects of a one-dimensional reading strategy, Durkin was reporting on the one- dimensional emphasis used in 42 kindergarten classrooms from 15 school districts.

Conclusion. A large portion of the reading or "reading-readiness" instruction was limited to learning isolated words through phonics and phonics worksheets.

Discussion. This same emphasis on "kindergarten phonics" is still required today by many school districts all over the country. A few cautions need to be presented:

- Phonics programs require much more use of word-by-word and letter-by-letter teaching approaches than the use of message approaches (such as dictating and reading their own simple "stories" about experiences similar to those of the main character in a "trade book" (also called "library book").
- As we just learned from Juel's study, some or many of the insecure students will stick like Super Glue to the overemphasized strategy, in this case, phonics.
- Consequently, some or many of those students will develop the habit of not searching for the author's meaning by using context clues and clues from their own past experiences.

There are further implications that can be made from both Juel's and Durkins' studies:

- Kindergarten teachers need to provide rich language and experience environments to balance a required heavy-emphasis phonics program.
- Better yet, the kindergarten teachers need time to prepare students for the abstract process called "phonics."

How? By teaching phonological awareness, using such playful procedures as oral rhyming and alliteration and by introducing games of blending and segmenting phonemes. In this way children are prepared through auditory patterns for subsequent mastery of "phonics," which requires the student to match auditory cues (phonemes) with visual cues (graphemes). In Chapter 3, on phonics, and Chapter 4, on phonological awareness, you will be given more information on this.

The First Grade Studies on "The Great Debate"

Bond, G. L., & Dykstra, R. (1967). The cooperative research program in first grade reading instruction. *Reading Research Quarterly, 2,* 5–142.

Discussion. The ongoing "great debate" (the message emphasis versus the word emphasis) did not begin with Durkin and Juel, of course. This debate was merely revisited in the 1960s and continues to this day. The famous Bond and Dykstra First (and Second) Grade Studies of the 1960s examined this issue by comparing the effectiveness of three types of programs: (1) phonics emphasis, (2) the teacher-controlled, whole-word, and student memorization procedure still used in most reading programs at that time, and (3) a precursor of the whole-language emphasis called "the language experience approach."

Conclusions

1. Teachers make the most difference, not the programs.
2. The language experience (message) approach produced test scores equal to those of the phonics and whole-word-memorization approaches.
3. Children who had been provided with the language experience approach tended to score higher on spelling.

The "Great Debate" Research of the 1960's

Chall, J. (1967). *Learning to read: The great debate.* New York: McGraw-Hill.

Chall made a major contribution to the debate by personally summarizing the results of fifty years of research. Notice how different her conclusion is from that of the First Grade Studies.

Conclusion. Early and explicit study of words and their letters was more effective than those approaches that emphasized meaningful messages.

Discussion. Because of the unprofessional quality of most of the studies she reviewed, I doubt that we can consider her conclusion to be valid or invalid. In spite of the massiveness of her review, as Chall admitted in her 1967 report, very few of the studies explained how the experimental and control groups were selected, how much time was given to each aspect of reading, how teachers were chosen, whether the quality of the teaching was similar for both control and experimental groups, and whether the teachers actually used the methods they were supposed to use. Thus, all but a few of the studies she examined were faulty in their procedures.

A further difficulty for Chall was the fact that the investigators seldom described the exact teaching procedures used in the study. Nor were statistical measures of chance provided by most investigators. With total truthfulness, and perhaps sadness, Chall was able to praise most of the researchers only for their sincerity in their attempts to find answers about what works best for teaching children to read. In her 1983 revision she amended her conclusions about early phonics because of what she had learned since the 1967 edition:

> It would appear, then, that an early opportunity to do meaningful connected reading in addition to learning how to decode is needed to integrate both abilities (Chall, 1983, p. 11).

Chall's major contribution did not turn out to be what her followers wanted it to be: a successful argument for early word study being more important than early message study. Instead it turned out to be a well-needed criticism of the research on reading that had been carried on before 1967. (Fortunately, this criticism seems to have had a significant impact on the quality of research reported and published since that time.)

A Major Refinement of the Great Debate Research

Corder, M. (1971). *An information base of reading: A critical review of the information base for current assumptions regarding the status of instruction and reading achievement in the United States.* Berkeley, CA: Educational Testing Service, Berkeley Office, U.S. Office of Education Project 0–9031, ERIC ED 054 922.

Corder agreed that Chall's body of evidence had been created by researchers who were not sufficiently prepared in sophisticated research and assessment methods. Therefore, he set up criteria that made it possible to select results only from reliable and valid studies. He and his colleagues then examined 1,855 "promising" research studies that were published between 1960 and 1970.

Results and Conclusions

1. A total of only 244 (13%) met the criteria and were accepted for description and analysis of their results.

2. The results provided by those 244 studies demonstrated no differences between methods of teaching reading that could not be attributed to pure statistical chance.

Discussion. The results of this study have probable implications for both teaching and research. This study, along with my own classroom observations, has convinced me that the degree of enthusiasm, wisdom, and freedom of a teacher is considerably more important than the program she or he is expected to use. My own observations and research have shown me that there are four factors that have more influence than the program:

1. How well and extensively teachers are prepared to understand and teach the reading process;
2. How skillfully the modeling of learning and communication processes is presented to the students;
3. How much opportunity teachers give themselves to uncover a particular individual's specific reading difficulties;
4. How much freedom teachers have (and take) to balance word study and message study.

Those four factors seem to make the most difference in how well students learn to read with enthusiasm and competence.

The Corder study reminds me also of three caveats that researchers and readers of research reports need to keep in mind:

1. The exact nature of the assessment devices used in comparative studies has a very large influence on the research results.
2. The degree to which assessments truly relate to the complex nature of the reading process is a major factor in producing valid research results.
3. Without validity and reliability of assessments, the results and conclusions can be very deceiving, and even self-serving.

Whole Language Advocates Join the Great Debate Research

Stahl, S. A., & Miller, P. D. (1989). Whole language and language experience approaches for beginning reading: A quantitative research synthesis. *Review of Educational Research, 59,* 1, 87–116.

Another extensive review of research was done by Stahl and Miller, who created a quantitative synthesis of the five projects involved in the First Grade Studies and 46 additional studies. Each study compared basal reading approaches, which emphasize phonics and sight vocabulary, to whole language and language experience approaches, which emphasize messages. In short, they analyzed the differences between programs that emphasized studying words and those that emphasized writing and reading messages.

Results and Conclusions

1. Message-emphasis [my terminology] was equal to word-study emphasis in the effects on standardized and nonstandardized test scores. This equality was also true for both achievement and

attitude measures, including classroom observations of the teaching and learning processes.
2. Whole language and language experience programs tend to be most effective when used with kindergartners and with others who need a reading readiness program, as compared to older students who are attempting to master the various decoding skills that lead to better comprehension.
3. For mastering the decoding of the spelling system, more systematic word study is probably needed to supplement what is provided through a message emphasis.

A Cognitive Psychologist's Study of the Great Debate

Adams, M. J. (1990). *Beginning to read: Thinking and learning about print.* Cambridge: MIT Press (Also Champaign, IL: Center for the Study of Reading, Report to the U.S. Office of Education.)

This exhaustive study by Adams was noted for its inclusiveness of a wide variety of evidence, including not only that from standardized test scores but also the results of eye movement studies, cognitive psychology studies, and other evidence relating to the learners and to the reading act itself.

Conclusions

1. Word recognition instruction is more effective when preceded by teaching neophyte readers to recognize individual letters accurately (p. 130).
2. When reading for comprehension, skilled readers tend to look at each individual word and to process its component letters quite thoroughly (based primarily on eye-moment studies, p. 102).
3. The ability to perceive words and syllables as wholes evolves best through complete and repeated attention to sequences of individual letters (p. 130). (This statement is not about the meaning of the words gathered through context.)
4. Predictive context increases people's ability and speed in deciding whether any given string of letters is or is not a word. *The more highly predictive the context is, the more it does so* (p. 139, emphasis mine).
5. Approaches in which systematic code instruction is included alongside meaning emphasis, language instruction, and connected reading are found to result in superior overall reading achievement (p. 49).

Discussion. Notice how Adams's first three conclusions emphasize word study, whereas #4 emphasizes message emphasis, and #5 emphasizes the necessary balance between word study and message study. You will find this balance emphasis if you read her hardbound version. You won't find that balance in the softbound summary edition. Perhaps this is because politics can sometimes influence the nature and results of large studies funded by state and federal governments as well as those funded by private foundations. I present this not as a negative indictment of such funding but as one of those "facts of life." We educators are just as human as anyone else.

For example, in the late 1980s in Champaign, Illinois, "The Center for Reading," a research center that has been a very productive, respectable, and valuable contributor to the cause of literacy, was asked by the U.S. Office of Education to carry out a major research study that would demonstrate the value of phonics in reading instruction. (There was a fear among many educators and parents, including myself, that phonics might be downplayed or ignored in the new whole language programs.)

Although concerned about the outcome of such a study, the Center agreed to take it on, perhaps in hopes that a new and thorough study would put an end to the Great Debate. The Center chose a noted researcher and cognitive psychologist by the name of Marilyn J. Adams to make one more attempt to test reality and free us all from the debate between the advocates of word-study emphasis and the advocates of message-study emphasis.

Adams's book showed a refreshing willingness to look at debate from a variety of vantage points. Dr. Adams made an intense effort to be objective rather than to simply please the funding Office of Education. The separately published paperback summary was developed by the Center, apparently to meet their obligations to the provider of government funds. Nearly everything in the summary edition provided exactly what the fund providers had asked for: praise for an explicit phonics emphasis from the earliest age possible. The more balanced approach recommended by Adams was not in the summary.

The Closely Related Debate about Reading Styles

Carbo, M. (1996). Reading Styles, *Educational Leadership, 53,* 5, pp. xx. Also Carbo, M. (1987). Reading Styles research. What works isn't always phonics. *Phi Delta Kappan, 44,* 5, 431–435.

During the 1980s Carbo developed a system of teaching reading that she labeled "Reading Styles." Her most important defense of this system was printed in 1987. This method consists of at least ten important instructional elements.

1. Observe each student and administer Carbo's questionnaire called *Reading Style Inventory.* This questionnaire asks young students about their attitudes toward reading and about their specific abilities related to different modes of learning to read, such as visual, kinesthetic, auditory, and tactile. (These four modes, for instance, would require such learning activities as using computers, typing, drawing, drama, active games, creating books, and following written directions for making things);
2. Match teaching methods to each student's apparent interests and abilities;
3. Demonstrate and model decoding and comprehension strategies;
4. Provide high-interest, well-written text;
5. Provide comfortable, relaxed reading environments;
6. Use choral reading and a variety of other group and individual reading activities;
7. Provide opportunities for students to write or dictate stories;
8. Have students listen to the teacher or a peer read aloud daily;
9. Provide time for students to listen to story tapes and follow along with the written version;
10. Combine the story tapes with the repeated reading technique.

Conclusion. Teaching toward students' learning styles is much more effective than "code emphasis" (phonics) methods, as long as all ten elements of the Reading Styles system are used.

Discussion. The Reading Style approach was developed by Carbo to counteract the heavy-handed word-study ("phonics first") emphasis that had become dominant in kindergarten and first grade classes (thanks only partly to the republication in 1983 of Chall's 1967 *The Great Debate*).

A contagious rash of doctoral dissertations was produced during the 1980s on the effectiveness or ineffectiveness of "teaching toward each student's style of learning to read." Thirteen of them won national awards for excellence, and most of them displayed impressive student gains, both in reading words (word recognition scores) and messages (comprehension scores).

It should be pointed out, however, that many of the dissertation studies used populations of students older than kindergarten or first grade. Some used populations of handicapped children. Thus, because of the age differences of the subjects, it became difficult to compare the results of a Reading Style approach with more traditional approaches. The older subjects were more likely to have mastered word decoding and were already much more involved in message decoding. The younger readers were probably still in a state of confusion about the value of word-by-word reading versus message reading. (For educational researchers, this became one of those apples and oranges dilemmas: How does one compare the two?)

Stahl Criticizes Carbo's Assumptions about Reading Styles

Stahl, S. A. (1988). Is there evidence to support matching reading styles and initial reading methods? *Phi Delta Kappan, 45,* 3, 317–322.

But now the new "subdebate" began. Stahl criticized Carbo's work by questioning the rigorousness of the research that seemed to prove that the meaningful (message study) approach of teaching toward students' learning styles was much more effective than "code emphasis" (word study) methods.

Perhaps most upsetting to Stahl was the low level of reliability of Carbo's *Reading Style Inventory,* ranging from reliability coefficients of 0.61 to 0.76, far lower than the usual assessment criterion of 0.90 or 0.95. He also felt that the validity of the students' responses to the inventory must be low as well. Why? Because the answers the teacher might want seemed to be much too obvious. Apparently, Stahl's real question became something like this: "Is this young student answering a certain way because he knows his own abilities and attitudes so clearly or because he is trying to figure out the way the teacher would like him to answer?" (This quote is mine, of course.)

Once Again: The Need for Balance between Word Study and Message Study

My own analysis of Carbo's research is that both Stahl and Carbo have the right answers, but perhaps for the wrong reasons. You and I previously examined two important conclusions of the First Grade Studies of the 1960s: (1) Children who experienced message-emphasis programs (Language Experience Approaches) did as well on the standardized tests as those who experienced a word-emphasis program; (2) It was the teacher rather than the program that made the greatest difference in the results.

Those conclusions have been reported many other times before and since the 1960s: The teacher's skill and attitude, along with the appropriate learning environment she or he provides, make the difference. Why should this conclusion be any different for the "reading styles" versus "code mastery" debate? For those educators who have spent most of their lives either teaching in school classrooms or observing people teaching there, this conclusion is definitely "no stranger."

What often happens when we read the Great Debate form of research studies is this: Our thinking about reading instruction tends to become polarized. Why? Probably because it's so much fun to take sides and to argue for our own pet teaching method. It's much more like work when we have to put so much energy into objectively studying the research while we're also busy observing and motivating our students.

In my forty years of observing and consulting with classroom teachers, I have found very few who are not willing to notice (or haven't already noticed) the virtues of balancing word study with real reading (message study). I've had numerous teachers tell me that they have shut their classroom door and balanced the curriculum to fit their students rather than follow only the dictates of the commercial and school district curriculum manuals.

Carbo's Success Revisited (Praise of a Different Color)

As for Carbo's success with her "teaching-toward-reading-styles approach," I feel the results she cites are to be expected. Yet, her conclusions may be granting far too much credit to the effectiveness of her *Reading Style Inventory* and her particular method of matching reading styles to reading methods. It's quite possible that Carbo may not be giving enough credit to the wisdom, flexibility, and enthusiasm of those teachers who have been successful with her methods.

Even more importantly, Carbo may not be giving enough credit to her intelligent choice of varied and novel methods that she has been blending into one coherent reading program. Specifically, she may not be giving enough credit to her multidimensional program. In addition to matching teaching methods to the learning styles of individual students, let me remind you that her program calls for at least ten instructional procedures, five of which I will present again, this time through the filter of the Great Debate:

- Careful observation of students (emphasis on learners as well as preplanned curriculum);
- Modeling major decoding and comprehension strategies (emphasis on both word study and message study);
- Providing high-interest texts that can be read and listened to at the same time (message emphasis);
- Using a variety of individual and group reading activities (balanced emphasis on message study and word study, as well as individualized and peer group learning);
- Providing comfortable relaxed reading situations (message emphasis).

To Conclude Our Examination of "Myth-Busting" Research

It is probably the wise balance of all those crucial elements that has led Carbo to her positive research results, and not just her attempt to match styles to methods. Perhaps what we can all learn from research and experience is that good reading instruction is not simply the provision of intensive word study. Nor is it merely the provision of practice in reading whole text. Good reading instruction might be better characterized as helping others in a caring and multihued way to gain information and entertainment from other caring people called *authors*.

Myth 1, Part C: Factual Case Study Illustrating Reading Problems that May Arise from a Student's Belief in the First Myth

The Case of Alfred, the Not So Great

Alfred likes to please adults in a variety of ways. He's always the one who volunteers to help kids in his classroom who are behind in their reading skill. In the first two grades he learned to read by either memorizing or faking words, and saying them fast when his turn came up to read a page in his reading circle. The teachers were pleased and seldom asked him to talk about the meaning of the authors' messages.

Now he's eight years old and in the third grade. His new teacher likes his compliance and helpfulness, but she's concerned about his inability to read without producing "false substitutes" (ineffective substitutions) and "no-shows" (a default, i.e., waiting for the teacher to tell him the word). He tends to make little sense out of the author's total message. Here's a sample of his reading, a very word-by-word process in spite of the fact that his new teacher prepared him by saying: "This is about turkeys and how silly they are. Why don't you read this to find all the silly things they do."

AUTHOR: Even with food all around, turkeys will not eat.

ALFRED: *Evven* with *fode* all around, turkeys will not eat.

AUTHOR: Turkeys can really be called "silly birds."

ALFRED: Turkeys can really be called "*city* birds."

AUTHOR: Many die from lack of food.

ALFRED: Many die from lack of *fode.*

AUTHOR: If they see anything bright, they try to eat it.

ALFRED: If they see anything *burnt,* they try to eat it.

AUTHOR: It may be a pencil, a small nail, or even a shovel.

ALFRED: It may be a (*no-show*), a small nail, or *evvan* a *shove.*

A Six-Step Assessment Model: Using Alfred as Our Student

This is one of the assessment models I'll recommend for use with your students. Please consider it a model you can easily modify.

____ **1.** Is this exactly the way he read it?

Answer: I checked the tape recording again, and it is.

____ **2.** Does he recognize instantly 90% of Fry's 100 most frequent "instant words?"

Answer: He read 93% correctly, reading each one in two seconds or less (see the Fry List in Appendix A).

____ **3.** Does he recognize at sight 80 percent of the common letter patterns (the visual part of graphophonics)?

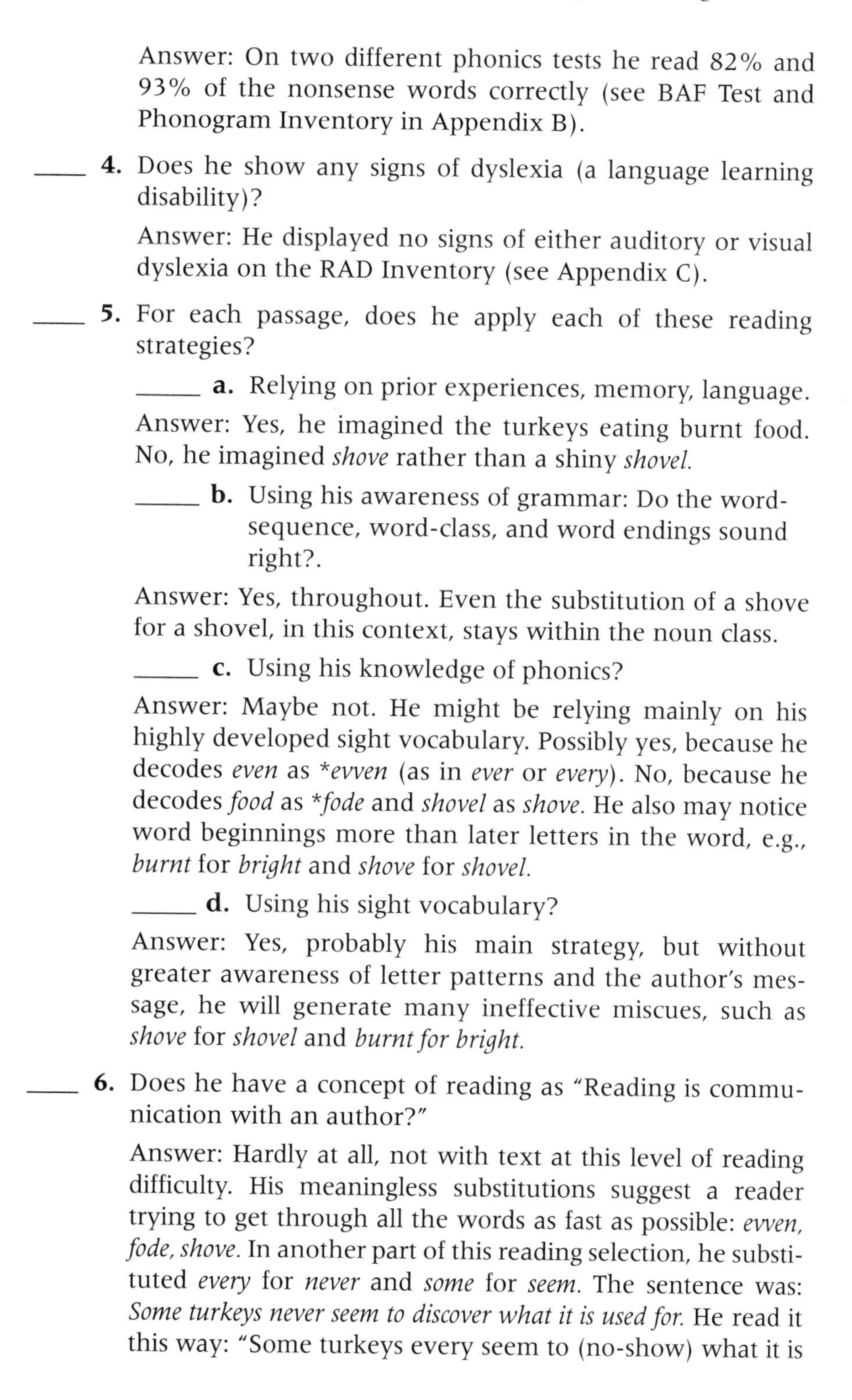

Answer: On two different phonics tests he read 82% and 93% of the nonsense words correctly (see BAF Test and Phonogram Inventory in Appendix B).

____ **4.** Does he show any signs of dyslexia (a language learning disability)?

Answer: He displayed no signs of either auditory or visual dyslexia on the RAD Inventory (see Appendix C).

____ **5.** For each passage, does he apply each of these reading strategies?

____ **a.** Relying on prior experiences, memory, language.

Answer: Yes, he imagined the turkeys eating burnt food. No, he imagined *shove* rather than a shiny *shovel.*

____ **b.** Using his awareness of grammar: Do the word-sequence, word-class, and word endings sound right?.

Answer: Yes, throughout. Even the substitution of a shove for a shovel, in this context, stays within the noun class.

____ **c.** Using his knowledge of phonics?

Answer: Maybe not. He might be relying mainly on his highly developed sight vocabulary. Possibly yes, because he decodes *even* as **evven* (as in *ever* or *every*). No, because he decodes *food* as **fode* and *shovel* as *shove.* He also may notice word beginnings more than later letters in the word, e.g., *burnt* for *bright* and *shove* for *shovel.*

____ **d.** Using his sight vocabulary?

Answer: Yes, probably his main strategy, but without greater awareness of letter patterns and the author's message, he will generate many ineffective miscues, such as *shove* for *shovel* and *burnt for bright.*

____ **6.** Does he have a concept of reading as "Reading is communication with an author?"

Answer: Hardly at all, not with text at this level of reading difficulty. His meaningless substitutions suggest a reader trying to get through all the words as fast as possible: *evven, fode, shove.* In another part of this reading selection, he substituted *every* for *never* and *some* for *seem.* The sentence was: *Some turkeys never seem to discover what it is used for.* He read it this way: "Some turkeys every seem to (no-show) what it is used for." As you can see, Alfred is not concentrating on the author's message. He is not picturing what the author is describing, nor is he concentrating on the letter patterns within each word. For example, *burnt* and *bright* have very different letter patterns following the letter "b," *urnt* versus *right.*

Obviously, Alfred needs your further assessment and follow-up instruction! (See Parts D and E of this chapter.)

Myth 1, Part D: Assessment Techniques Needed to Determine Whether a Student Is Using a Reading Strategy Based on the First Myth

Symptom Check List* for ____________________ Date __________

____ **1.** Reads with word-by-word style

____ **2.** Relies mostly on word-study strategies:

_____ correctly reads author's words that are part of sight vocabulary

_____ but substitutes sight words for similarly spelled words

_____ pays attention only to first letter of word

_____ pays attention to first few letters but not to last few letters

_____ produces "no-shows" (defaults; teacher must give him the word)

_____ produces "false substitutes" that don't fit author's meaning

____ **3.** Creates meaningless miscues by not searching for author's messages:

_____ Shows this through "false substitutes," e.g., *bird* for *bead*

____ **4.** Declines to predict the next word on the basis of context

____ **5.** Unable to accurately retell or discuss the passages read

*You may wish to read Chapter 2 (on miscues) before you actually use the following assessment and intervention techniques.

Other Assessment Tools

1. Use The Six-Step Assessment Model found in Part C. If you suspect that your student has the wrong concept of what reading really is, write several messages to each other, calling him either "author" or "reader" depending on his role at the moment and let him do same to you.
   For example:

   "Hi Alfred, the Reader. How long did you sleep last night?"
   Yours truly,
   Miss Jones, the Author

   "Hi, Miss Jones, the Reader. I slept nine hours. How about you?"
   Yours truly,
   Alfred, the Author

2. If miscues (mistakes) occur with simple sight words, check sight word awareness by using a portion of the Fry Word List in Appendix A. If a student misses more than 10% on the list, use sight word games and other activities described in Myth 3, Part E, as part of the gradual improvement process.
3. If miscues occur because of obvious lack of awareness of spelling patterns and corresponding phonics patterns, check phonic pattern awareness by using the Baf Test and Phonogram Test in Appendix B. If the student misses more than 10% on either list, use games and other activities similar to those described in Myth 3, Part E, as part of the gradual improvement process.
4. If student is producing false substitutes, see Myth 1, Part E, for the training guide, A Collaborative Procedure for Teaching Students How to Catch False Guesses.

Myth 1, Part E: Positive Intervention Procedures Designed to Help Students Learn to Read Messages rather than Only Words

1. Don't correct them or use any other negative intervention when they use strategies that effective readers use, such as:
   a. Predicting words incorrectly and then self-correcting in order to stay with the author's message
   b. Using substitutions that have the same meaning as the author's words

c. Using omissions or insertions to put the author's true message into their own way of speaking
d. Repeating a word or phrase in order to have the time to glance forward or backward to obtain greater message clarity and/or word accuracy

2. Correct them only:
   a. At the end of a sentence or paragraph
   b. When they "default" (a "no-show," waiting for you to tell them the word) or substitute a word for the author's word that does not fit the author's message. Ignore other types of miscues (see Myth 2, Part A, for explanation of this procedure).
   c. By teaching or reminding them how to self-correct (see the training document that follows as a Model Training Procedure).

CFG: A Collaborative Procedure for Teaching Students How to *C*atch *F*alse *G*uesses

Introduction

Although the following teaching procedure is used in this case with only one student, this procedure can be easily modified for use with more than one student. You and I will start with a review of the types of word substitutes that students make when they read. (*Substitute* is less abstract and generally a more understandable word for young children than the word *substitution*.) In the following sentence, why does Jennifer first use *pernet* and then *permanent* as substitutes for *permit*?

> They went to the ranger station to get a *pernet,* I mean *permanent,* to cut Christmas trees.

Isn't it mainly because she has yet to learn that reading is searching for the author's message? Isn't it because she is concentrating only on one word at a time rather than on the author's messages? Substitutes like the ones Jennifer created provide both teacher and student with small peepholes for viewing the particular belief that a student has about the nature of reading.

If the substitute is one that maintains the meaning of the author, this is normally a sign that Jennifer understands the author's message and is reading for meaning. If the substitute is one that ignores or distorts the essential message of the author, this is generally a sign that Jennifer is not reading for meaning but is simply trying to survive in an uncomfortable situation. How? By plugging in real or nonsense words that get her quickly through the passage.

CFG Step One, Lesson One: Explain the CFG (Catch *F*alse *G*uesses) Procedure to the Student

(Suggestion: You can just read the script, word for word, the first time, using the ellipsis (...) as your signal to pause for your student's response. After that, it would be better to treat the script in a more conversational style.) The first step is to explain the CFG procedure.

> What we're going to do now is much like detective work.... You and I will work together to find clues and catch suspects. (Continue to prepare them for detective work.)
>
> When good readers read, they search for clues just like detectives do.... The clues help the good reader guess the next word! Did you know that? ...Most of the time we make good guesses, but sometimes we don't. Isn't that right? ...If we make true guesses we understand what the author is saying to us. But if we make false guesses we don't understand what the author is saying.... Am I right? ...So what do you think we should do if we make a false guess of the next word? ...Yes, we simply fix the false guess.
>
> But how do we fix it? ...Okay, we fix it by being good detectives who try to find out what went wrong with our first guess. Does that make sense? ...So, good detectives, and good readers, both do two things: They keep looking carefully for clues, and they find out what went wrong with their first guess and fix it. Okay, now see if you can tell me two things that good detectives and good readers both do. (Help them practice saying those two ideas before going on.)
>
> ***How To Fix Your Guess***
>
> Now, let me show you how to be a good detective and a good reader. We'll start by using one of the things that detectives have to use all the time. They use a tape recorder, don't they. They use a tape recorder to listen to the plans of the criminals...or to record a criminal's confession...or to report on how well the case is being solved.... Did you know that?...
>
> So, what else do detectives use besides a tape recorder? ...Do you know? ...Yes, and they also might use a magnifying glass to check out very small clues...like a human hair...or maybe a greasy

fingerprint.... Then they try to find out whose hair it is—or whose fingerprint it is, right? ...

CFG Lesson One: First Practice Session on Catching False Guesses

The teacher now reads out loud a paragraph or two from a selection you have already copied for Jennifer's use, or from the selection below. (The student must have her own copy of what you are reading.)

As you read to Jennifer, produce at least three types of substitutions. One substitute should be a good substitute, such as a synonym for one of the author's words, e.g., *house* instead of *home.* One substitute should start with the same letter or two but not relate to the author's message, e.g., *hose* instead of *home,* and one substitute should be a nonsense word **hommy* instead of *home.*

Tell her not to correct you until after you finish reading. She should just circle each word that you miss. (Note that for your copy each substitution you should produce is in bold print and not italics. Her copy should include only what the author said.)

First Example of False Substitutes

Student's Copy: Roberta felt something strange crawling down the bare skin on her back. It was something like a spider, or maybe a flying ant. She reached over her shoulder and tried to slip her fingers around it.

Teacher's Copy: Roberta felt something strange crawling down the bare skin on her back. It was something like a spider, or maybe a **frying** ant. She reached over her **shood-er** and tried to **put** her fingers around it.

After you have read this short passage to Jennifer, let her tell you which words you missed and why she thinks you missed each word.

CFG Lesson Two: Recording and Analyzing Session

Your student "will now prepare some information for your later detective work." Have her read a passage of about 100 to 300 words depending on her age and ability. If she produces either a false substitute or makes it necessary for you to tell her a word (a no-show) more than ten times during the first one hundred words, you need to find an easier selection for the rest of this particular recording.

If she produces fewer than two false substitutes or no-shows during the first hundred words, you need to provide her with a more difficult selection for the rest of her recording.

After the Recording Move on to More Detective Work

Then move on to "more detective work," giving Jennifer a copy of "Who Stole the Teacher's Lunch Box?" along with a small magnifying glass for her "detective work."

Second Practice on False Substitutes

Introduce the story: The title of this story is "Who Stole the Teacher's Lunch Box?" Just by reading the title of the story, I would like you to guess how it's going to end. Okay, now I would like you to search for three things while you are reading the story. I'll read them to you twice and then you tell me the three things you're going to look for in the story:

1. See how good your guess was for the ending of the story.
2. See who you think was the best detective in the story.
3. See if you can be a good detective and figure out why Alfred made his reading mistakes (shown in bold type, not italics).

Now, you're going to look for how good your guesses were about how the story ends, who is the best detective in the story, and why Alfred made his reading mistakes. So tell me the three things you're going to look for in this story?

All right, here's the way we're going to play this detective game. You read Alfred's sentence right after I read the *author's* sentence. Understand? Then, right after you read Alfred's sentence, you get to be the detective and find out why Alfred made a false guess! Are you ready?"

*Who Stole the Teacher's Lunch Box**

AUTHOR: The teacher, Mr. Frankenstein, stared at his students.

ALFRED: The teacher, Mr. Frankenstein, **starred** at his students.

AUTHOR: "Who took my lunch box?" he said. "I need to eat!"

ALFRED: "Who took my lunch box?" he said. "I **want** to eat!"

*Please read the directions that follow the story before beginning your session of alternate reading.

AUTHOR: Suddenly he saw his lunch box under Patty's desk and marched toward her like an angry policeman.

ALFRED: Suddenly he saw his lunch box under Patty's desk and **marked** toward her like an angry policeman.

AUTHOR: Mr. Frankenstein reached down and picked up a hair on top of the lunch box. "This is the color of your hair," he said to Patty, "so you must be the one who took my lunch box!"

ALFRED: Mr. Frankenstein reached down and picked up a hair on top of the lunch box. "This is the **collar** of your hair," he said to Patty, "so you must be the one who took my lunch box."

AUTHOR: Patty turned her head toward her friend, Bob, and laughed. "Hey Bob," she said. "Your hair is just as blonde as mine is—even though it **is** full of dirty oil."

ALFRED: Patty turned her head **to warn** her friend, Bob, and laughed. "Hey, Bob," she said. "Your hair is just as **blue** as mine is, even **thought** it's full of dirty **oh-ill.**"

AUTHOR: Patty then picked up the lunch box and felt the oil on it. "Bob should be your main suspect," she said with a smile.

ALFRED: Patty then picked up the lunch box and felt the **oh-ill** on it. Bob should be your **man suss-pet,**" she said with a **snail.**

Directions for Analyzing Substitutions

After the student reads each sentence the way Alfred did, have her use the magnifying glass to enlarge both the author's word and Alfred's mistake at the same time. How are the letters in the word from the author different from the letters in the word read by Alfred?

After discussing the letters, move on to the author's message in that sentence: Now that you, Detective X (Use student's actual name), have studied the letters close up, you need to look far away into your imagination. Why? Because a detective's job is to find out things like: Exactly where is the hair located? On the floor? Which part of the room? Near Mr. Frankenstein's desk? Where was Mr. Frankenstein?

And remember, the detective not only has to find clues, he or she has to think about each clue, like: Why is that hair in that particular place? Could it be a hair from the head of someone in the classroom? How will I find out?

Now then, a person who is reading has to look at the *big* picture too. You have to look at the whole sentence if you want to know what the author is telling you. Is that right?

Now that you've looked carefully at the letters and words, raise your magnifying glass so you can see the whole sentence. Try reading the same sentence that Alfred read and say the word *blank* (or "empty space") instead of saying what Alfred said (*starred* for *stared*).

Does the word that Alfred used fit well in that empty space? Does the sentence make any sense that way? Does it fit the big picture the author was trying to make for you? What was that big picture in the first sentence? What was happening, do you think? (The teacher must have been staring in an angry way at the students.) Okay. So what word should Alfred have used instead of *starred."*

What were the two things that went wrong when Alfred read that first sentence? Yes, his guess didn't make sense. People don't star at each other. They stare at each other, right? So his guess didn't make sense. And what was the other thing that went wrong for Alfred? Yes, he didn't look at the letters carefully enough.

Examine the other false substitutes that Alfred created in the same way, making sure that you and the student (s)always check both kinds of mistakes: (1) not making sense (to reader or author), and (2) not looking at the letters enough. Finally listen to her recording, preferably on the following day, using the same methods of determining the false substitutes and how to fix them.

In Chapter 2, you will learn more about miscues and the only two you need to watch for.

CHAPTER 2 The Second Myth of Reading

Myth 2, Part A: Poor Readers Make the Most "Mistakes" (and Teachers Should Correct Those "Mistakes" Immediately)

Let's move on to our second myth: "Poor readers are those who make the most mistakes, and its corollary, good readers seldom make mistakes." A first-born offspring of this belief is a teaching myth, one supported by our understandable need to "monitor" our students' reading progress. It goes like this: "Every reading mistake that a student makes should be immediately corrected," a belief once strongly supported by many psychologists.

Let's check the validity of those two "biologically" related myths. Here's a tough validity question for you: Which of the following mistakes, (called miscues) do you think good readers will produce more often than poor readers? (*Poor readers,* a very relative term, are those who use unsuccessful strategies in attempting to understand what an author is saying. "Good readers" are those who use successful strategies in attempting to understand what the author is saying.)

Which of these four miscues will most good readers produce more often than most poor readers?

Self-corrections? My father drives our car too fat...no, too fast.

Insertions? He drove the car to *our* church.

Omissions? He drove our car to (the) church.

True Substitutes? He drove our (automobile) *car* to church.

Did you predict that at least the first and last ones (self-corrections and true substitutes) are used more by good readers than poor readers? If so, you are right:

Good readers do self-correct their mistakes (miscues) so they can understand what the author is saying. And, remember, in order to make the author's message more understandable, good readers may subconsciously substitute a similar word of their own for the author's word.

But Why Do Good Readers Miscue?

Of course, good readers don't consciously produce miscues. Instead, they take advantage of their marvelous brain, a very fast "computer" and one that allows them to predict what words and ideas are coming next. (This is true whether we are reading or listening.) What's more, our brains are very flexible computers. So flexible, in fact, they allow us, with the help of our vision system, to use several strategies simultaneously, whether reading silently or out loud. Here are just a few of the simultaneous strategies good readers use.

> Predict words and ideas that are coming up soon—pronounce a previous word aloud while looking at the following words.
>
> Confirm our predictions by examining both context and letters—self-correct our predictions or other miscues as we read.
>
> Find spelling patterns in each word that allow us to recognize it correctly—pronounce words that we recognize (or predict).

In Part C of this chapter, you'll be able to watch a student use those strategies. For now, I'll be happy if you're merely amazed at what power you have when you use your mind.

The Stunning Power of the Mind

But why did our student substitute the word *car* for the word *automobile*? Was it because he didn't notice that the spelling of *automobile* and *car* are quite different? No, that's not very probable.

Eye movement studies done in the 1960s have shown that his substitution more likely came about because his eyes were busy glancing at the words ahead. At the same time, his mind was storing *automobile* and translating that word into the familiar word *car*.

Okay, But What about Omissions and Insertions?

"Surely," you might be thinking, "omissions and insertions are used more by unsuccessful readers than by successful readers. Right?" No, omissions and insertions are used more by successful readers. Why do they use them more? Unconsciously, in order to make the author's language more like their own. In short, they often omit and insert words in order to understand and personalize the author's message. Remember these examples?

Author's Version	**Insertion**
He drove the car to church.	He drove the car to **our** church.
	Omission
He drove our car to **the** church.	He drove our car to church.

How about the Miscue of Repeating a Word?

I'll answer that question with another question: Why do poor readers and good readers alike repeat a word? Is it because they're not sure of how to pronounce it? Sometimes. But more often they're using "a repeat" to give them more time for looking either ahead or behind to determine the author's meaning. For example, one reader repeated two words as she read this sentence: *"She felt in the* ***dark****...*dark for **the...** the magnificent diamond." She revealed in my "think-aloud" session with her that she repeated the word **dark** in order to glance at the surrounding five words, "She felt in the for," and determine the author's exact meaning of **dark.** (My generous dictionary just informed me that there are at least twenty-one definitions for *dark.*) In this same sentence the reader repeated the simple word *the* in order to gain a few seconds to study the hard words coming up, *magnificent* and *diamond.*

Having students think aloud while they read has convinced me that this strategy of looking ahead and behind for meaning occurs quite often. But why did she bother to repeat the words *dark* and *the*? Why not just pause to think instead?

The Art of Stalling (for a Purpose)

We all use different forms of stalling when we're speaking or reading. How many times have you found yourself saying "and uh" or "so uh" when you're speaking? Or how about "uhmmm" or "well, uh." Or perhaps you prefer to stall by just repeating a word or phrase you just said. "This theory is profound ...profound...And uh, the reason is..."

And yet, what's our purpose for stalling like that? I know what you're thinking: "We repeat in order to keep others from getting a turn to talk." True! True!! But just as often, we repeat because (pause) we need time to think, time to problem-solve by using strategies that allow us to understand what we mean—or, in written communication, what the author means.

The Parallel Wiring inside Our Heads

So uhmm, what's the general...uh, idea that I'm trying to communicate to you? Simply this: Our flexible, problem-solving mind can arrive at the author's meaning by doing several things at once, rather than one thing at a time. Our brain, thank goodness, has "parallel wiring" instead of "serial wiring."

Let me use an analogy: In the World War II days of the 1940s many people were still using "serial wiring" for their Christmas tree. That is, they basically had only ***one wire*** leading to a bulb, then leading on to the next bulb, and then the next, and so on. The problem? When one light burned out, ***all*** the lights went out. So now what did they have to do in order to determine which light had burned out? What most people did was to try a **new bulb,** which they had to exchange with the bulb in each socket, ***one at a time,*** until all the lights went on again.

By the time the fifties arrived (the "Happy Days" period) most people had switched to parallel lighting for their Christmas tree. Because there were now two independent wires connected to each bulb, running alongside each other like a two-lane road, the electricity could complete its path, even if one of those diggynabbed, #%$&* lights burned out.

To put it more simply, two things could happen at once: The electric current could keep on flowing, and the good lights could keep on glowing. With the brain, of course, we're not limited to only two "parallel wires." Most of us are not limited even to the number of lanes (going and coming) on a typical California freeway.

Do We Teach Reading as a Single Wired Process?

Alas, fair Juliette, we teachers and parents, in order to be kind to our students, have attempted to simplify the learning of the reading process. How? By keeping them on a serial path, moving "through" each word, one at a time, hoping the lights will keep on burning and enlightenment will come to us at the end of the path.

But that way, when our students arrive at a word they don't know, the whole message burns out! (We're now in the dark.) So...to deal with that problem, the well-meaning teacher or parent provides them, not with the new light bulb, of course, but with "the new word." Perhaps when we do this to neophytes, we imagine them learning this caution: Do not to make a single mistake, or the lights will go out (the enlightenment will not take place). In that way, though, we deprive them of the chance to use their flexible, multilaned minds. Instead, they have to please us whenever they're asked to read out loud. Of course, afterwards, if they're brave enough, they go off to a corner and read like thinking readers do, by

- Predicting and confirming predictions;
- Miscueing and correcting miscues;
- Subconsciously changing words into more familiar synonyms;
- Searching for spelling patterns and their corresponding sounds;
- Doing whatever it takes to understand the author.

Fortunately, many students learn from their own experience that "to miscue is to take risks that often lead to understanding." (This is just as true with reading as it is with life, itself—maybe.)

All Right. So When Should We Correct Them?

Should you correct your student's "mistake" before she even has a chance to do her own self-correcting? Even before she has a chance to realize that the word she used doesn't make sense in the sentence? Please don't, I beg you. Remember, instead, this four-beat chant:

> The reading task is problem solving:
> A chance to learn—HOW to think!
> Oh say it's time to toast with drink.
> 'tis a break, right? for all mankind,
> A victory for the human mind!!

Should You Let Students Correct Each Other's Reading "Mistakes"?

Let me recommend a more productive learning procedure: If you're working with more than one student, make a chart of rules that explain the learning behavior you want.

Rules of Learning Together

1. Each student has the right to first correct his own mistake.
2. Each has the right to substitute his own word for the author's, if it works.
3. If the substitute doesn't work, the teacher will help the student at the end of the sentence to think about the message.
4. We learn together best by watching others learn from their own mistakes.
5. We learn together best by praising each other for good thinking.
6. Our goal is not to finish the story now but to improve our reading skill. (Give them time right afterward to finish the story on their own.)

Which Miscues Should You Help Each Student Correct?

As you will see in Parts B and C, it is generally a waste of time to help students correct any miscue but a false substitute (a substitution that doesn't make sense) or a no-show (the student "defaults" by letting the teacher provide her with the word). Those two miscues are the only miscues that are consistently accepted by unsuccessful readers and seldom accepted by successful readers. You can save a great deal of time by either ignoring or encouraging all four of those miscues that good readers produce as part of their eager attempt to understand the author.

In Conclusion

Here is my summary statement for this part of the chapter. You might want to sit down and sip on a double cappuccino while you read the next caution. As much as you possibly can, without suffering guilt, save teaching and learning time by ignoring these miscues:

- Self-corrections (unless you want to praise this strategy)
- One-word or two-word omissions
- One-word or two-word insertions
- Repetitions of a word or phrase

Instead, both teacher and student can spend much more time on:

no-shows and false substitutes.

Myth 2, Part B: Research That Refutes the Second Myth

A Study on Teachers' Distortion of the Meaning of *Reading*

Davinroy, K. H. et al. (1994). "How does my teacher know what I know? Third graders' perceptions of math, reading and assessment." Colorado, Clearinghouse #TM021949. Publication Type: 143;150.

Results and Conclusions

1. The children in this study felt that a teacher's praise is applied mainly to such performances as good handwriting and punctuation, or good reading aloud with expression (instead of the "search for meaning)."
2. By third grade children usually recognize reading as a search for meaning but this understanding often becomes distorted by the monitoring (assessment procedures) of their teacher.

Discussion: I have found those two observations to be true with children and adults of all ages. They have been motivated to "put on a show" more than concentrating on their strategies of understanding the author's messages. My colleagues, graduate students, and I have found that both children and adults tend to put on a "good show" by reading each word quickly, correctly, and with expression (even when they don't really understand the message they're reading). I guess we've trained them too well.

Study of Teacher-Made Constraints on Students' Reading

Harste, J. C., & Carey, R. F. (1984). Classroom constraints and the language process. In J. Flood (Ed.), *Promoting reading comprehension* (pp. 30–47). Newark, DE: International Reading Association.

Conclusions:

1. What the teacher believes about the nature of the reading and learning processes determines the strategies of reading taught to the students.

   Discussion: Let me give you an example. If the teacher believes strongly that "learning to read requires correction of each word that a student reads incorrectly," he will probably teach word correction more than meaning correction. He will probably be tempted to count all miscues as mistakes to be immediately corrected.

2. A teacher's belief can become what is called a "learning barrier," unconsciously but firmly inserted between the teaching and learning processes—thus limiting what students can learn.

Consider these as examples of learning barriers: (1) having students concentrate on one word at a time rather than predicting the author's message, (2) correcting every mistake immediately, and (3) counting all types of miscues as "incorrect reading strategies." Those three learning constraints can lead to what Frank Smith refers to as "tunnel vision." As I have seen so often, this tunnel vision causes many students to limit their reading strategies to phonics and/or the recall of sight words.

Consequently, those three learning barriers introduced by teachers—(1) concentrating on words more than messages, (2) correcting too soon, (3) counting all mistakes as equally important—may easily cause the reader to ignore the contextual clues provided by his own memories of past experiences: listening to stories, reading books, and engaging in his own adventures.

By concentrating on students' word mistakes instead of message mistakes, many neophytes have been taught to concentrate too much on correct words and too little on correct interpretation of authors' messages. The result of this is students who fail to develop "pictures in the mind" as they read. Unless students search for such pictures as they read, much of what they read is meaningless and forgettable.

It is not surprising that students have usually scored higher on word tests and lower on comprehension tests. Most likely they have been sufficiently prepared to recognize and pronounce words, but insufficiently prepared to picture what the author is talking about. Thus, they can't remember enough about the passage to choose the correct answer for the test question. Yet, it's our fault, not theirs. We've been unwittingly giving them the wrong message about the real purpose of reading.

Study on Substitutions and Self-Corrections

Beebe, M. J. (1979–1980). The effect of different types of substitution miscues on reading. *Reading Research Quarterly,* 15, 324–336.

Results and Conclusions:

1. Those students who self-corrected their "false substitutes" (kids' language for ineffective substitutions) or used substitutes that fit the meaning of the passage had the highest scores on both silent reading comprehension and on their ability to retell the passage read.
2. With this fourth-grade population the best readers (top 20% on silent reading comprehension) corrected about twice as many false substitutes as the poor readers (bottom 20%).
3. Teachers should focus a large portion of their concern on miscues that interfere with comprehending the author's meaning.
4. Analysis of oral reading miscues is an effective way of inferring silent reading miscues.

Discussion: The #4 conclusion is very important in helping us realize that by teaching students how to correct the two consistent poor reader miscues, no-shows and false substitutes, we can significantly enhance their progress in comprehending what they read silently. Also, by observing how they handle no-shows and false substitutes, we can make frequent assessments of their concepts of and strategies for reading.

1. Are they improving in their awareness that reading requires a search for the author's meaning?
2. Are they developing both effective comprehension strategies and word recognition strategies for this search?

Further implications of Beebe's study may be that three major aspects of reading skill—concept for reading, strategies of comprehension and word recognition, and an improved level of comprehension—can be best developed first through oral reading instruction and assessment. Shortly after an oral reading "strategy session," students should apply what they have learned to silent reading, paired reading, or journal and composition writing related to the passage read.

This is ***not*** to say that everything they learn about reading must begin with an oral reading lesson. Once students have learned a reading concept or strategy, they can extend that concept or strategy through both silent and oral reading, in either order. It is a good idea, of course, to extend the concept or strategy through the contrasting experiences of less difficult and more difficult text. Less difficult text (and plenty of it) will build up their self-confidence. More difficult text will challenge them to keep on improving their skill (much like the very gradual raising of a high-jump bar challenges an athlete).

Research Review on Self-Corrections

D'Angelo, K. (1982). Correction behavior: Implications for reading instruction. *The Reading Teacher, 35,* 395–398.

Results and Conclusions:

1. Second-grade good readers corrected a significantly greater percentage of miscues than poor readers.
2. Good beginning readers corrected three times as many substitutions as poor beginning readers.
3. Poor readers concentrated on correcting graphophonic miscues more than message miscues, and this was done more often than good readers did it.
4. Good readers corrected a greater percentage of miscues than poor readers, whether reading at frustration or instruction levels.
5. Good readers, compared to poor readers, paid more attention to both syntax and semantics while making corrections.
6. Good readers, compared to poor readers, corrected twice as many miscues that changed grammatical structures (such as tense, syntax, number, and case.)
7. Self-corrections seem to be good predictors of a high level of comprehension and retelling scores.

Discussion: Once again, we see that the study of miscues, rather than a reliance only on asking recall and inferential questions, can provide teachers with an accurate and direct way of monitoring and assessing a student's comprehension strategies. (See Chapter 5 for more on comprehension.)

Study on Insertion and Omission Miscues

D'Angelo, K. & Mahlios, Marc. (1983). Insertion and omission miscues of good and poor readers. *The Reading Teacher, 36,* 778–782.

Results and Conclusions:

1. Insertions and omissions changed the author's meaning less than 3% of the time.

2. Those two types of miscues, combined, represented less than 8% of all miscues.
3. When their research subjects did use insertions or omissions, 99% of the time the author's meaning was not sacrificed; 93% of the time the author's syntax was not sacrificed.
4. Both poor and good readers used insertions and omissions only occasionally.
5. Time spent on analyzing omissions or insertions could easily be omitted. That way, more attention can be given to (ineffective) substitutions and to (praising) self-corrections of (ineffective) substitutions.

Another Study on Omissions and Insertions

Goodman, K. & Gollasch, F. (1980–1981). Word omission: Deliberate and non-deliberate. *Reading Research Quarterly, 16,* 6–31.

Results and Conclusions:

1. The frequency of substitution, omission, and insertion miscues is in the order shown in the present sentence.
2. Omissions tend to be a way of reducing redundancy or (simply not voicing) words that are well known.
3. Insertions actually increase as a reader becomes more competent.
4. Omissions usually demonstrate that the reader is communicating with the author (by using the reader's own experiences with language).

Study on Qualitative versus Quantitative Analysis of Miscues

Goodman, Y. M. (1972). Reading diagnosis—qualitative or quantitative? *The Reading Teacher 25,* 32–37.

Conclusions Quoted:

In a discussion of research from 1962–1972, Yetta Goodman presented these conclusions:

1. "When a reader's errors are simply counted and this quantitative information is used for placement, the reader may be encouraged to read material which is either too simple or too difficult for him" (p. 32).

2. "By placing a premium on error counts, a teacher begins to believe that minimizing miscuing behavior is desirable. Such is not the case" (p. 32).
3. "The number of miscues a reader makes is much less significant than the meaning of the language which results when a miscue has occurred" (page 32).
4. "To simply count miscues is to short circuit a complex process." (p. 37).

Research Review on Effects of Text Difficulty on Miscues Production

Leu, D. (1982). The analysis of oral reading errors. *Reading Research Quarterly, 17,* 3.

Results and Conclusions:

1. When low ability students are given text to read that is too difficult, they are likely to produce miscues based more on graphic similarity (e.g. "He ran to his bridge" for "He ran to his bride"). In contrast, high-ability students reading the same selection are likely to produce miscues based more on semantic similarity (e.g., "He ran to his new wife" for "He ran to his new bride)."
2. The ease of reading a text can make a significant difference in whether a reader uses more of a graphophonic strategy or a semantic context strategy.

Discussion: I recommend checking out the ideas in Part B by applying them to the following case studies.

Myth 2, Part C: Case Studies Illustrating Reading Problems That May Arise from the Second Myth of Reading

The Case of Jack the Repeater

In first grade, Jack's reading instruction consisted of phonics worksheets and basal reader stories that were read word-by-word. In second grade he was considered to be a "poor reader" who relied entirely on the strategy of "sounding out words."

In third grade he was tested for dyslexia and judged to be free of learning disabilities. This evaluation caused the teacher to treat him as a "regular student" who just needed individual help in using context as well as phonics. By fourth grade Jack had discovered that "reading is like listening to someone else talk." His teacher in fourth grade capitalized on that discovery by letting him pause to think as often as he wanted to. His rendition of the following story included five miscues: four repeats and one no-show:

> The people at the...**at the** rodeo stood up.
> They were all waiting for...**for** the big ride.
> Everyone came to see Bob...Hill ride...**Midnight** (a no-show).
> Midnight is the best horse in the show.
> He is big and fast. Midnight is...**is** a black horse.
> Can Bob...**Bob** Hill ride this great horse?

Which one of those five miscues would you consider to be a "serious miscue" that would require your comments and assistance? How many of the five miscues were simply "stall-to-think strategies?"

Jack, the Subsitution Expert

By the end of fourth grade Jack's teacher considered him to be "a person who comprehends what he reads." This was most evident to her when Jack read silently. When Jack read out loud, the teacher had to keep reminding herself that substitutions are often an indication of a reader trying to understand the author's message, but in his own words. Here is an example of his changing the author's version only enough to help him understand the author's message.

The Conestoga Wagon

AUTHOR: People riding in wagon trains **did** not have **our** easy **ways** of traveling.

JACK: People riding in wagon trains **do** not have **their** easy **way** of traveling.

AUTHOR: Their **trip was** made in what was called a Conestoga wagon.

JACK: Their **trips were** made in what was called a Conestoga wagon.

AUTHOR: These were good wagons, but they were not comfortable.

JACK: These were good wagons, but they were not comfortable (same as author).

AUTHOR: **They had broad** wooden seats.

JACK: **The hard boards were** wooden seats.

What are you thinking? Yes, he really did read it exactly that way. Does he seem to understand this story so far? Has he changed the author's message in any significant way? Which type of reading cue is he relying on the most, phonics or meaningful context? Can you consider him a good reader yet? (Would he be an even better reader if he were to create and confirm his predictions on the basis of both phonics and context?) As one answer to that last question, let's look at one more sentence that occurred later in the story.

AUTHOR: When this old wagon reached a river the wheels were **removed.**

JACK: When this old wagon reached a river the wheels were **moved.**

His substitution of *moved* for *removed* changed the author's meaning considerably. The author wanted Jack to picture people *removing* the wheels so that "the wagon" could be "made into a flat boat." The picture that Jack created of people just moving the wheels missed the author's point, and caused Jack to stumble through the rest of the story. A use of both phonics and context would have avoided the sudden drop in his understanding of the author's message.

Nevertheless, Jack is becoming a good reader because he searches for the author's meaning. We need to help him, and others like him, to balance their strategies in their search for meaning. How to do this? Try using the techniques described in this chapter when you get to Parts D and E.

Jacklyn, the Girl Who Puts It All Together

In Part A, I promised you the opportunity of watching a good reader who has learned to use her flexible multilaned brain in a simultaneous way. Here are reading strategies similar to the list in Part A:

1. Look ahead at words to predict ideas and words that are coming;
2. Pronounce a word (or synonym);
3. Confirm your predictions by examining both context and letters;
4. Self-correct your predictions or other miscues as you read;

5. Find letter patterns in each word that allow you to pronounce it correctly.

Watch Jack's sister, Jaclyn, as she skillfully reads this selection. (Please observe the numbered strategies she uses and match them with the list above).

AUTHOR: America's rainy green Northwest is noted for its fabulous forests.

JACLYN: America's rainy green Northwest is **noted...** noted for its fabulous forests. (By glancing back at the previous list you'll see that Jaclyn used strategies 1, 3, and 5).

She repeats (stalls on) the word *noted* in order to look ahead and/or to remember what she has already read. Because the author has already told her that the Northwest is rainy and green, she is now busy using context to predict what the Northwest could be famous for. (Something that is grown there? A plant that is green? Could it be trees? Could the trees be tall because of all that rain?) At the very same time, she is busy examining the letter patterns in each word or syllable (no-ted for its fab-u-lous for-ests).

AUTHOR: Every time you look up **you'll** see tall stately **firs** and cedars.

JACLYN: Every time you look up **you will** see tall stately **fires...**no, firs and cedars (Strategies 1, 2, 3, 5).

As she looks ahead, Jaclyn's brain stores the word *you'll* and translates it into "you will," (which is the way she normally pronounces it out loud). At the same time, she glances fleetingly at the next words to follow; "you'll see tall stately firs and cedars". Using both context and letter pattern cues, she then self-corrects *fire* for *fir* in her mind and immediately self-corrects out loud.

Before you go on to the next section see if you know which context and phonic cues Jaclyn probably used for the last part of the second sentence: "you'll see tall stately firs and cedars". Can you see what cues she used from both sentences to self-correct *fire* to *firs?* ...What context cues (*forests, look up, tall stately*)? What letter patterns in the words or syllables (*you-'ll, s-ee, t-all, st-ate-ly*)? Perhaps you'll agree with me: The human brain can be a very fast and flexible computer.

Myth 2, Part D: Assessment Techniques Needed to Determine the Use of Strategies Based on the Second Myth of Reading:

A List for Teacher's Self-Evaluation ____________________
Date ________

______ **1.** Considers self-correcting to be interfering with smooth reading

______ **2.** Usually counts omissions as reading errors

______ **3.** Considers a repetition to be a sign of stress or unawareness

______ **4.** Usually counts insertions as reading errors

______ **5.** Counts any miscue that "interferes" with smooth reading

______ **6.** Counts all or nearly all substitutions as reading errors

______ **7.** Thinks that reading music and books are very similar acts (i.e., "both words and notes require the same precision of expression")

______ **8.** Praises students the most for reading without making mistakes

______ **9.** Corrects each reading mistake immediately after each word

______ **10.** Encourages students to correct each other immediately

______ **11.** Uses word recognition tests more than message comprehension tests

______ **12.** Believes that dialect differences are really reading errors

______ **13.** Trusts "established" scoring methods of commercial tests more than own personal observations, particularly of whether or not a student's substitution relates to the author's meaning

Symptom Check List for Student: ____________________ Date ________

______ **1.** Slowly reads word by word to be sure each word is correctly decoded and pronounced

______ **2.** Defaults (waits for teacher to give word) to avoid making a mistake

______ **3.** Declines to predict the next word on the basis of context

______ **4.** Often misses the total meaning of the author's message

______ **5.** Considers himself to be a poor reader because he makes so many word mistakes

______ **6.** Declines to predict what will happen (or will be said) next

______ **7.** Has difficulty retelling a story or another type of message

______ **8.** Hates to read out loud in front of other students

______ **9.** Prefers almost any subject or activity to reading

Other Assessment Tools

1. Select from the Six-Step Assessment Model found in Myth 1, Part C. Modify the steps to fit your particular assessment problem.
2. Check Other Assessment Tools in Myth 1, Part C. It is quite likely that some or all five of those tools will be appropriate in this case.
3. Use individual assessment of the responses of poor readers when you praise them or use highly specific feedback (see Part E for examples).

Myth 2, Part E: Positive Intervention Procedures Designed to Help Students Overcome the Effects of the Belief That Only Poor Readers Make Mistakes (which should be immediately corrected, of course)

Should you intervene? Of course. You're the teacher. But intervene positively and at the end of a sentence or paragraph.

1. Praise poor readers with specific feedback whenever they use any of the following strategies of good readers:
   a. Self-correcting based on author's meaning and word's letter patterns;
   b. Using substitutes that fit into the meaning of the author's total message;
   c. Using omissions to put author's words into reader's speaking manner;
3. Using insertions to put author's words into reader's speaking manner;
4. Repeating to gain time to obtain greater word or message accuracy.

Some Specific Examples of Praise

AUTHOR: Every time you look up you'll see tall stately **firs** and cedars.

STUDENT: Every time you look up you'll see tall stately **fires**, no, **firs** and cedars.

Self-correcting: Good for you! You realized that *fire* doesn't make sense but *fir* does. What else did you check so you could come up with the correct word? Yes, you checked the letters of the word and you realized that f-i-r doesn't spell *fire*.

AUTHOR: He drove our **automobile** to church.

STUDENT: He drove our **car** to church.

True substitutes: I like the way you substituted the word *car* for *automobile*. You changed the author's word into your own word.

AUTHOR: He drove our car to church.

STUDENT: He drove the car to **our** church.

Effective insertions: You slipped in the word *our* between *to* and *church*. Is that because you were reading that sentence the way ***you*** would say it? That's just fine. It shows me that you understood what the author said.

AUTHOR: He drove our car to **the** church.

STUDENT: He drove our car to church.

Effective omissions: Okay, you left out the word *the* before *church* but the sentence still makes sense. Do you think you changed the author's idea when you left out the word *the*? No? Then it's perfectly all right to read it the way you did. Let's go right on to the next sentence.

AUTHOR: Everyone came to see Bob Hill ride Midnight.

STUDENT: Everyone came to see Bob...**Bob** Hill ride Midnight.

Effective repetitions: I'll bet I know why you repeated the word *Bob* in that sentence. You said it twice so you would have more time to think about what the author was saying in the whole sentence. Am I right?

5. Model The Self-Correction Strategy for your student or students by thinking out loud as you read. For example: "

   Okay, listen to me think out loud as I read the next sentence to you: Every time you look up you'll see tall green **fires** and cedars." Wait a minute. *Fires* doesn't make sense. The author is telling me about ***forests,*** so he must be talking about different kinds of trees. Cedars are one kind of tree, but ***fires*** are not a kind of tree at all. Oh, yeah, it's not **fires.** It's **firs.** It's spelled f-i-r, not f-i-r-e. The author is telling me about forests that have fir trees and cedar trees in them. It's a good thing I checked the letters, isn't it? Now I know why fires didn't make sense. It doesn't fit what the author was talking about.
6. There are more ideas in Part E of Chapter 1 that will reinforce the ideas for intervention in this chapter. Just adapt them in ways that fit your student(s).

CHAPTER

3 The Third Myth of Reading

Myth 3, Part A: All Phonics Methods Are Equally Effective

Have you ever been told by politicians or reporters that school teachers don't consider phonics to be important? If so, maybe you've come to the same conclusion I have: Politicians win votes and reporters receive bonuses by stirring up the public that way. This, in spite of a 1998 U.S. national survey, showing that 99 percent of the elementary school teachers in the United States considered phonics to be "important." Two-thirds of those teachers considered phonics to be not only important but "essential."

Different Definitions of Phonics

With that said, we can now examine an even more serious myth: "All methods of teaching phonics are equally effective in helping neophytes to read." Research and personal experience have demonstrated that this notion can be detrimental to a student's learning how to read, and to wanting to learn how to read. It's true that there are several methods by which English speaking neophytes (both child and adult forms) can learn "phonics." but, some of those methods have the effect of changing the student's goal from "learning how to read" to "learning how to survive those phonics lessons."

Please join me to search for clues as to why this is so. And while we're doing that, please keep in mind that each method of teaching phonics is based on a different definition of what phonics is. We'll begin our observations with the most simplistic of those definitions.

Method 1: Sounding Out. Definition: "Phonics is just sounding out words one letter at a time."

Example: "cabin" = kuh + aahhh + buh + ihh + nuh

*Advantages of the Sounding Out Method**

At best, this method provides neophytes with a very primitive way of learning phonics from those adults who are unaware of phonics methods that are much easier, more accurate, and less puzzling.

Disadvantages of the Sounding Out Method

1. Once you "sound out" each letter separately, you have to blend all those so called "letter sounds." This may be possible with *bat* which represents the phonemes /b/ + /a/ + /t/ but it's not possible with *that* which represents the phonemes /th/ + /a/ + /t/ rather than the "letter sounds" /t/ + /h/ + /a/ + /t/.

(Phonemes are the smallest language sounds, like /th/ + /a/ + /t/)

2. Treating phonemes as independent sounds makes the blending process quite difficult unless your students have already been trained in phonological awareness.

Phonological awareness includes the ability to imagine both the separation of phonemes within words and the blending of those phonemes back together. You will learn much more about phonological awareness in Chapter 4.

But why is the "sounding out" method difficult for students who have not been trained in phonological awareness? Partly because sounding out each letter into its corresponding phoneme creates extra phonemes for your blending task. For instance, the sounding-out method of pronouncing *cabin* would be: cuh + aahh + buh + ihh + nuh. Try saying the b-sound without creating two phonemes, /b/ [buh] + /u/[uh], regardless of how softly or quickly you say it. If you sound out the word *cabin* that way, you will produce eight phonemes rather than five:

/c/ + /u/ + /a/ + /b/ + /u/ + /i/ + /n/ + /u/ (vowel sounds all short)

*Note that I'm talking about the primitive "sounding out each letter" method. I will discuss the "synthetic phonics" method separately.

Neither pronunciation is terribly meaningful (unless you have a picture of a cabin right in front of your eyes). You might know what a cabin is, but what is a *ka-aba-inna,* for Pete's sake? Okay, so it's difficult for students to use the sounding-out-each-letter method of phonics. Are there any other reasons why this is so?

3. About a fourth of the individual English speech sounds (phonemes) are represented by two or more letters, e.g., t-h in **thin,** s-h in *shine,* p-h in *phone,* k-n in *knife,* g-h-t in *knight.* This situation can make the sounding-out method a "knightmare," causing you to sound out each letter in *knight* like this: kuh + /nuh + I + guh + huh + tuh (which to some novices must sound very much like a chant we sang in kindergarten, proudly accompanied by our homemade, oatmeal box drums):

"kunna-Iga-hutta kunna-Iga-hutta kunna-Iga-hutta"

4. Also, it takes so long to "sound out" each and every letter that the sense of the author's context and meaning can be lost in the pages forever. If you don't believe me, try sounding out each letter, one at a time, in the following sentence. Go on, try it. I dare you: "On the ***night*** I met the ***knight,*** I had a terrible ***fright.***"

> (Words 1 to 3): Ah-nuh...tuh-huh-uh...nuh-I-guh-huh-tuh.... Okay, that's enough. A better idea is to wait till we come to Method 4, The Phonogram Method, for a much easier, more visual way to begin learning to decode rhyming words (even words like ***night, knight,*** and ***fright.***)

Method 2: Synthetic Method. Definition: "Phonics is a process that includes: (1) naming *graphemes* by "their sounds" (phonemes); (2) learning to represent each phoneme in writing with one or more letters; (3) blending those letter/sounds into a meaningful word we use in speech; (4) representing each word/sound in writing. For example,

1. *thanks* can be written: *th a nk s*
2. *th, a, nk,* and *s* are called /th/ + /a/ + nk + s. Each phoneme is pronounced or imagined in isolation

3. these sounds are blended to achieve the pronunciation of /thanks/
4. the sound /thanks/ is written as *thanks*

A Sample Lesson, Using the Synthetic Method (simplified example)

(Teacher writing the letter b on the board) "Here's our new sound for the day. This sound is **buh** (pronounced in a breathy manner with very little or no vibration). "Say this sound with me. Say it to your partner. Say it to me. Good."

"Now I'm drawing a little ring around /b/. And now I'm drawing a big ring around the little ring. Let's put some sounds that you already know right inside this big ring. I'm sure you know this sound /a/. What is it? Yes, it's the aahh sound. Give me a word that has the /a/ sound in it. Good, *nap* has the /a/ sound in it Now I'm going to put another sound that you know inside the big ring. What is it? Yes, it's the /t/ sound.

"Now we're going to make a word out of those three sounds. First we'll write the "buh" sound on the board /b/. And now you write the /b/ sound on your paper. While you're writing it, I'll walk around and give you help if you need it. Very well done, you guys. Now let's write the next two sounds right after the /b/ "buh." First the /a/ (in *cat*) and now the /t/ "tuh."

"Good. You have all written the buh, the aahh, and the tuh sound correctly on your paper. Now let's say each one slowly: buhhhh-aaaahhh-tuhhhh. Good. Now say them a little faster: buhh–aahh–tuhh. Now say them all together very fast: /b/ + /a/ + /t/. That's great. So how do we say this word, Sally?

"You're not sure? All right, say it slowly with me. Good. Now say it faster. Say it fast. That's right, Sally, it's */bat/.* Our new word is *bat.* Everyone say our new word. Now everyone write our new word three times on your paper. Now say the word three times to your partner."

As you can see from this example, there are approximately four steps in the teaching process for the synthetic (putting together) method:

1. The teacher has the students say the new sound.
2. The students now write the new sound (as a single letter like *c* or a digraph like *ch*).
3. Now they blend the new sound with known sounds.
4. Then they write the blended sounds as a new word.

In brief, the sequence is from SAYING the sound, to WRITING the sound, to BLENDING the sounds, and to WRITING the blended word. (Say-Write-Blend-Write).

Advantages of the Synthetic Method

1. This method seems to be more concrete and less abstract than the analytic method (of taking words apart). (The analytic method is coming right up.)

2. It appears to be a useful direct and explicit teaching approach, especially for inexperienced readers who cannot handle the more abstract "discovery" methods. In this sense it can be useful for novices who are new to English.

3. Research results generally favor the synthetic method over the analytic method, but under the following conditions: (1) when researchers are comparing only the two methods that emphasize the auditory learning mode: the analytic and synthetic methods; (2) when their student population has not had the opportunity to learn the more visual phonogram method (also called "the onset-rime method" or "analogy method"); (3) when the student population is mostly enrolled in an ESL program (English as a Second Language).

4. Having your students write the letters and words makes it easier for them to recognize those letters and words in the future, because writing provides both a visual and kinesthetic (bodily motion) mode to balance the auditory mode. All three modes thus enhance the student's memory.

5. Unlike the "sounding out method" the synthetic method does encourage the pronunciation of blends (bl, cl, dr, fr) in a combined way, i.e., in a /bl/ instead of /b/ + /l/ manner. It also handles the digraphs in a combined way, i.e., in a /th/ way rather than the /t/ + /h/ way.

Disadvantages of the Synthetic Method

1. This method, without skillful teaching, may provide learners with the false notion that each letter represents a consistent sound. In the real world, each of the vowel letters (*a, e, i, o, u, y*), as well as some of the consonant letters (*c, s, ch, t, g, p, k, h*), represent a variety of language sounds. Here are some examples with which you are already familiar:

The *a* in *cap* has a very different sound from the *a* in *cape,* in *may,* or in *wait,* not to mention the variety of sounds represented by *a* in *care, caught,* or *father,* or even that dreaded word, *dead.* The confusion over the letter *a* is bad enough. But the bafflement increases profoundly when you come to *e.* The sound of *e* is represented in at least fifteen different spellings, e.g., *read, feed, even, Caesar, receive, receipt, people, demesne, key, machine, yield, debris, amoeba, quay, sadly.* You can see the possible problem you can have in teaching learners to associate a single sound for each vowel letter in isolation.

1. There is no one consistent sound connected to each vowel letter. Nor are there always consistent sounds connected to the letters called "consonants." Just look at: *c* in *city* or *cat; s* in *sand* or *his; ch* in *church* or *school; g* in *girl* or *giant; p* in *penny* or *phone; k* in *king* or *knight;* or even *t* in *tiny* or *nation.* No wonder kids sometimes think we're lying to them.

2. The synthetic method can be painfully boring to moderately advanced readers and especially to those who prefer to devote their reading time to observing and discovering the world of fiction and nonfiction on their own rather than being told, explicitly and directly, "We're going to call this letter 'buh.'" (This, of course, is not a disadvantage of the synthetic method but a disadvantage of using the same reading program with every individual.)

3. This highly auditory synthetic method, if used too soon in your reading program, may take instructional time away from learning the quicker, more meaningful process of recognizing visual letter patterns in rimes and onsets.

4. The highly explicit and direct synthetic method may create the habit of learning only by being told rather than learning just as often through the essential thinking processes of discovery and experimentation.

5. Unless learners have had abundant phonemic awareness experiences with the English language, the synthetic method can require too much time to learn, not to mention the time in the future to unlearn what they have mistakenly learned about vowel letters, vowel letter patterns, and some of the consonant letters. (What one of my very young students had learned was this: "There are good letters [consonant letters] and bad letters [those naughty vowel letters with their variable sounds].")

Method 3: Analytic Method. Definition: Phonics is a method of breaking up a word into its initial, medial, and final graphemes and phonemes, then analyzing them in relation to other letters and sounds in the word.

This direct teaching method requires students to learn each grapheme–phoneme connection through "discovery." The student is not explicitly told the language sound represented by one or more letters. Instead she or he is asked to observe a cluster of words and to discover which letters and sounds are the same in each word.*

> I'm going to **church,**" said **Chuck.** "I'm going to play **chess,**" said Nancy. "Well, I'm going to the **beach,**" said Tyrone. "And I'm going to **munch** on potato **chips,**" said Reyes. So they **each** did their own thing.

A Teacher's Lesson Plan, Using the Analytic Method

Watch each word as I read the story on the board. Now let's write a list on the board of all the words in that story which have the same two letters that *church* has. (*church, Chuck, chess, beach, munch, chips, each*). What two letters do they all have? (*c* and *h*) Now let's read those seven words together to hear which sound is the same in all those words. Yes, it's /ch/. Everyone say that sound. Okay, now we'll read the whole story together; then each of you can read one of the sentences.

As you can see, there are generally five steps in the analytic teaching process:

1. The teacher reads the words in the context of a complete story.
2. The target words are separated from the story for word analysis.
3. The students are challenged to discover what letters are the same in each of the target words.
4. The students are challenged to discover what language sound is the same in each of the target words.
5. The students and teacher return to reading the whole story in order to place the words back into context.

*Please read the "story," then examine the learning/teaching processes used for the "analytic method."

In brief, the sequence is from CONTEXT, to SEPARATION, to same GRAPHEMES, to same PHONEMES, and back to CONTEXT.

Advantages of the Analytic Method

1. Students can gradually learn the correspondence between a phoneme and its representative grapheme. More importantly, they can learn those correspondences in the natural linguistic context of whole words, sentences, and stories.
2. The analytic method provides the context of a story rather than an isolated way of learning or reviewing initial, medial, and final graphemes and phonemes in a word.
3. The analytic method provides opportunities for observation and discovery, two thinking skills that need to be developed for use in our careers and our everyday survival.
4. The analytic method allows students to collaborate with their peers in the learning and discovering processes.

Disadvantages of the Analytic Method

1. Instruction with this method seems to be not explicit, auditory, and direct enough for those students who learn best through a more auditory mode.
2. The analytic method requires the learner's considerable energy and concentration necessary for the valuable but difficult processes of observation, analysis, discovery, and classification.
3. The discovery process can be done by only one person, with the other learners merely copying the discoverer. (The person who is teaching needs to have students take turns in the observation, analysis, discovery, and classification processes.)
4. Many students seem too inexperienced to think abstractly about language (e.g., by noticing or creating classifications like "letters that are the same in different words" or "sounds that are the same in those different words").
5. Many students need sufficient prior *oral* language experiences with the concepts and procedures involved in the acts of observing, analyzing, discovering, and classifying before attempting to learn the nature of phonic cues. It's often easier to first learn those thinking procedures through speaking and listening, and then apply them to the more abstract processes of reading and writing.

6. Many students need a background of concrete, enjoyable language play, phonemic awareness activities, and inventive spelling before they can successfully analyze someone else's written language in abstract, categorical ways.

Method 4: Phonogram Method. Definition: "Phonics is a process of making a comparison or analogy between two rhyming clusters of letters like *lap* and *flap*. The reader who already knows the word *lap* and the letter blend *fl* (as in *fly*), can now reason that the new word, *flap*, must rhyme with *lap*."

Note that the rhyming part of *lap* and *flap* consists of the letter cluster, *ap*. This cluster of letters is referred to in writing as either "phonogram" or "rime." The word-spelling, *rhyme*, refers to the sound of the rime or phonogram. The letters *l* in *lap* or the *fl* in *flap* are referred to as "the onset." The phonogram method, then, is one that requires breaking up a word or syllable into its onset and its rime (or phonogram). The following are some examples of the phonogram method. For example, if you come across an unknown word, *shack*, you can first associate the phonogram **ack** with words you do know, like ***back***, *Mack* and ***sack***. Then you attach the sound for *sh* (learned from words like ***she***, ***shell***, and ***dish)*** to the sound of **ack** and pronounce the word correctly as *shack*. In other words, you create an analogy between the new word, *shack*, and the known word, *back*. Here are some other examples of analogies between new words and known words (the rimes are in bold type).

Letters in New Word		**Sounds in Known Word**
t h i n = th + **in**	as in	w i n = /w/ + /in/
g r a m = gr + **am**	as in	ham = /h/ + /am/
s t r a p = str + **ap**	as in	trap = /tr/ + /ap/

> Linguists refer to **am, ut,** and **ap** as rimes (or phonograms), which are identical spelling and sound patterns at the end of several words or syllables, e.g., ***but*/*but*-*ter*, *lap*/*lap*-*ping*, *ram*/*ram*-*ble***. They refer to **fl, gr, str, b, h,** and **tr** as *onsets* (letter and sound patterns at the beginning of rhyming words or syllables, e.g., ***lap***, ***flap***, ***flap ping***, ***flut ter***.

Advantages of the Phonogram Method

1. With only thirty-seven ending rimes (ending phonograms) you and your students can generate over 500 words used frequently by children in grades 1 through 3: ack, ail, ain, ake, ale, ame, an, ank, ap, ash, at, ate, aw, ay, eat, ell, est, ice, ick, ide, ight, ill, in, ine, ing, ink, ip, it, ock, oke, op, ore, ot, uck, ug, ump, unk.

2. With each of those thirty-seven final phonograms (and forty-seven others), you and your students can creatively generate ten or more words that are frequently used by neophyte readers, e.g., **ack** leads to *back, hack, Jack, lack, pack, quack, rack, sack, tack, black, clack, crack, knack, shack, smack, snack, stack, track,* and *whack,* twenty words for the price of one phonogram, all of them with a stable spelling pattern and short vowel sound /a/. If I could acquire just one share of **ack** on the stock market, I'd buy it.

3. Both phonograms (rimes) and common vowel patterns are easily learned at the same time through the use of T-frames. Three of the T-frames, filled with rhyming words, are displayed below.

FIGURE 3.1 Family-Word Charts Using a T-Frame

	VC		VCC		VCE
	in		ink		ine
p	in	m	ink	d	ine
t	in	p	ink	f	ine
w	in	s	ink	l	ine
ch	in	bl	ink	m	ine
gr	in	dr	ink	sh	ine
				sp	ine

Notice that each T-frame contains words that have the same final phonogram (on the right of the vertical T's trunk). This final phonogram must be spelled exactly the same in each word included in that T-frame. This sample of three T-frames is representative of frames for five vowel patterns and eighty-four phonograms. Each of those eighty-four phonograms (rimes) can generate anywhere from ten to twenty rhyming words.

Using the phonogram phonics method, over 1,000 words may be quickly learned, associated with at least nine other rhyming words, and easily remembered by association. The learning of phonograms can also lead to skill in the analysis and recognition of longer words with two or more syllables. For example, the learning of the three-syllable word *animate* can be recognized from the common phonogram **an,** (as in *can, Dan,* and *fan*), ***im*** (as in *him, Tim,* and *slim*), and **ate** (as in *late, Kate,* and *date*) **an-im-ate.**

4. At the same time your students are learning all those final phonograms (rimes), they are also shopping for letters (t), digraphs (th), and blends (tr) to go with the rimes. All those letters, digraphs, and blends are called "onsets." As you know, the word *onset* means *beginning.* So, let's go shopping for onsets that go with our rimes, and see what kind of outfits (words) we can come up with.

How about purchasing the common onset **st** (as in *stone* or *stop*) to go with the common rime **ick** (as in *sick* or *lick*). Put them together and what do we have? We have *stick,* a winner, and it goes very well with your purchase of *tick, trick* and *thick.* Now we've moved from thirty-seven phonograms, to eighty-four phonograms, to hundreds of long words that contain those eighty-four phonograms, to thousands of combinations of onsets and rimes. A great shopping trip!

5. In case you're lost, we're still in the middle of our list of advantages of the phonogram–phonics method. Another advantage of this method is that students almost universally enjoy the challenge of creating the rhyming "family words" that center around a single phonogram. (The family words are those that you saw in each T-frame. Each family word has the same rime but a different onset, as in the **ight** family: *br***ight,** *f***ight,** *fl***ight** *fr***ight,** *he***ight,** *l***ight,** *m***ight,** *n***ight,** *r***ight,** *s***ight,** *t***ight.** (This list would be developed spontaneously, not alphabetically. Call it "The Bright Family" or whatever your students want to name it.)

6. The learning of rimes and onsets is a pleasant and powerful way for students to learn not only how to read but how to spell.

7. Research shows that it is considerably easier for students to identify phonograms than it is to identify isolated vowels, e.g., c + ape is much easier to recognize than c + a + p + e. Thus, with phonograms, students can immediately recognize the correct vowel sound for this particular *a.*

8. The learning of rimes and rhyming words allows students to begin adapting patterned book compositions similar to "The Cat and the Hat." For instance, they can write or dictate their own group book called "The Bat and the Gnat." (For people who live in the frozen north, a gnat is a small biting fly, a favorite dish for bats and birds.) Your students might enjoy creating a story conflict similar to that of Tweety and Sylvester.

9. For thousands of years, human beings have relied on rhymes to enhance their memory of historical events, everyday duties and experiences, names, drama lines, stories, songs, wise sayings, and poetry. Auditory rhymes and visual rimes (phonograms) can be very powerful tools in developing literacy.

Disadvantages of the Phonogram Method

1. The phonogram method emphasizes visual learning more than auditory learning. Students who rely more on the visual mode of learning may need supplementary practice with the analytic method.

2. Students who rely more on the auditory mode for learning may need supplementary practice with the synthetic method.

3. Relying solely on the phonogram method may deprive some students of the chance to truly master phonics as a tool for decoding and understanding the messages of authors.

4. Like all phonics methods, the phonogram method requires previous (or at least concurrent) direct lessons on phonemic awareness. Without those lessons many students will be left in the dark as well as left in the dust, with respect to learning phonics. Phoneme awareness lessons followed by onset and rime lessons may be the best way for inexperienced readers of the English language to learn how to segment and blend phonemes for purposes of reading or writing.

Method 5: Definition. In its advanced form, phonics requires the search for common vowel patterns in words, i.e., the vowel pattern method.

Rather than search only for phonograms in each unknown word, more advanced students can search for the common vowel patterns found in phonograms, syllables, and words. One of those common vowel patterns can be found in words like ***in,*** p***in,*** ***ed,*** ***bed,*** ***at,*** *sc**at,*** ***up,*** *c**up,*** *cab-**in,*** and *rob-**in.*** All of those words and syllables are dependent on the vowel–consonant ending. All of them use "the vowel–consonant pattern." Children as well as my university students, prefer to call it the "V–C pattern" rather than the traditional CVC pattern, because VC fits those words and syllables that are also common phonograms, *at, Ed, am, an, it.*

Each of those words demonstrates the type of word that is very likely to have a short vowel sound. We know just by looking at the phonogram in *bet,* which is **et,** that the *e* will have the short vowel sound. The short vowel sound similarly exists in the vast majority of words, syllables, or phonograms ending in the VC pattern, such as *th**at**, j**et**, sp**in**, sl**ob**, c**up**, mark**et**, **in**val**id**, r**ob**bing.*

Likewise, the visual rimes (phonograms) in these words or syllables—**amp,** *lamp;* **ent;** *tent;* **ick,** *sick;* **ock,** *sock,* **ump,** *slump*—all have the same vowel pattern, the vowel–consonant–consonant pattern (or for children, "the VCC pattern"). Each of those words has a short vowel sound.

However, just by looking at the phonogram in *beak,* **eak,** we know that the **ea** digraph will have the long vowel sound that exists in a large number of words or syllables ending in the VVC pattern, such as long **a**—*p*__ain,__ long **e**—*b*__eam,__ long **o**—*g*__oat,__ long double **o**—*s*__oon,__ and the two-syllable words like *bab*__oon,__ *rem*__ain,__ *str*__eam__*ers,* and *fl*__oat__*ing.*

Teaching Phonogram and Vowel Pattern Connections

The phonogram method, as it is gradually becoming mastered, leads to the more sophisticated vowel pattern method. To help you understand the transition from the phonogram method to the vowel pattern method, it is important for you to scrutinize two charts called "Sample Words for Teaching Vowel Patterns" (Figure 3.2) followed by "The Phonogram to Vowel Pattern Connection" (Table 3.1). This is the easiest way for you to understand the five consistent vowel patterns, based on the 1000 most frequent words in the English language.

FIGURE 3.2 Sample Words for Teaching Vowel Patterns

	VC		VVC		VCE
	in		ink		ine
p	in	p	ink	m	ine
w	in	w	ink	w	ine
ch	in	th	ink	sw	ine

TABLE 3.1 The Phonogram–Vowel Pattern Connection

Short Vowel Sound Patterns: VC and VCC
in pin...at rat...top cop...bun fun...pet bet = All VC
ink pink...ash cash...rock sock...rust must...send bend = All VCC

Long Vowel Sound Patterns: VCE, VVC, and CV
ape cape...rope hope...(rare with "e" and "u")...like hike = All VCE
eat heat...boat coat...mail jail...(rare with "i" and "u")... = All VVC
he she...so go...my try...(rare with "a," "i," and also "u,")... = All CV

Advantages of the Vowel Pattern Method

1. The phonogram method, while it is being mastered, can gradually lead to the mastery of the more inclusive and abstract *vowel pattern method.*

2. The vowel pattern method allows for more abstract thinking by tying together all of the 100 or so common phonograms (rimes) into only five consistent vowel patterns. Thus, it becomes the most efficient tool for vowel sound analysis. (Most words not fitting the five patterns can be handled as separate "phonogram kings" and their attending family words, e.g., **ar** in *car, bar, tar,* or that renegade, **ead,** in *dead, lead,* and *tread.*)

3. The vowel pattern method provides the most accurate method of determining whether vowel letters in a word represent the short or long sound of the corresponding phonemes.

4. This method allows the reader to recognize short or long vowels without memorizing every single rime.*

Disadvantages of the Vowel Pattern Method

1. The vowel pattern method requires more abstract generalization that the phonogram method. Skill in using the VC vowel pattern,

*Those words that can not be decoded through one or more of the regular vowel patterns, can easily be decoded through the use of phonograms that do not have either a short or long vowel:

> **ay** in *day* and *hay,* **all** in *ball* and *call,* **ar** in *car* and *far,* **are** in *care* and *dare,* **ark** in *dark* and *mark,* **aw** in *paw* and *jaw,* **ear** in *dear* and *fear,* **ew** in *few* and *grew,* **ight** in *fight* and *might,* **ind** in *find* and *mind,* **ow** in *low* and *slow,* **ow** in *cow* and *how,* **ore** in *core* and *chore,* **orn** in *torn* and *worn.*

from my own experience in teaching it, requires the mastering by sight of about three phonograms each for short a, e, i, o, and u (for a total of fifteen phonograms). However, remember, that phonograms can be taught gradually from an early age through exposure to rhyming games and verses. Formal teaching of phonograms can be blended with the vowel patterns by using the "vowel pattern frames" shown earlier on page 59.

2. The vowel pattern method may not lend itself to complete mastery before the age of eight or nine.

3. The vowel pattern method can take longer to learn and even be too difficult for learning disabled or ESL students.

Myth 3, Part B: Research That Refutes the Third Myth of Reading

A Review of Research Results and Conclusions on Phonics Instruction

Stahl, S. A., Duffy, A. M., and Stahl, K. A. D. (1998). Everything you wanted to know about phonics (but were afraid to ask). *Reading Research Quarterly, 33,* 3, 338–355.

Conclusions and Implications

1. The methods of teaching phonics have been influenced primarily by *the beliefs that reading educators have had about the nature of reading:* a process of recognizing words or recognizing messages; the process is therefore primarily dependent on phonics or primarily dependent on the reader's simultaneous use of four cueing systems: phonics, grammatical structure, semantics (an author's word meanings), and schematics (a term derived from *schemata,* meaning a person's prior experiences condensed into her interpretations of those experiences.)
2. Phonics instruction should include the alphabetic principle that the letters represent the spoken language, including phonemes, spoken words, and spoken messages. Progress in learning this principle can be determined through students' whole-text reading, the way they listen and respond to text, and their invented spelling—by *observing in each case whether they understand that words have both meaning and sound.*

3. Phonics instruction should include instant recognition of letters, a skill that should be learned both in isolation and in connection with text reading and meaningful writing.
4. Phonics instruction should not include word pronunciation rules, but instead should concentrate on sequential grapheme–phoneme patterns, such as those spelling sequences called "rimes" or "final phonograms."
5. Phonograms and other coupled spelling–phoneme patterns can be mastered through abundant practice, particularly through searching for and recognizing spelling patterns in complete and interesting text.
6. Examples of spelling patterns need to be presented in clusters at first (or created by the learners). *Students need numerous examples of each pattern, such as those in predictable patterned stories* (and in family-word charts created by the students).

A Study of Different Phonics Emphases in Preschool, K, 1 and 2

Morrow, L. M., and Tracey, D. H. (1997). Strategies used for phonics instruction in early childhood classrooms. *The Reading Teacher, 50,* 8, 644–651.

This study involved seventy-six classrooms that were observed regarding the nature of phonics instruction at four different levels: preschool, kindergarten, first, and second grades. The classrooms were in districts of varied socioeconomic, racial, and ethnic backgrounds. A total of 722 observations of phonics instruction were recorded and analyzed.

Results and Conclusions:

1. Contextual (functional and meaningful) lessons or minilessons on phonics occurred 72 percent of the time in preschool, dropping down to 33 percent in kindergarten, and dropping even further to 21 percent in grades 1 and 2 combined.
2. Explicit lessons (discrete phonics concepts taught directly and with worksheets) occurred 19 percent of the time in preschool, jumping up to 56 percent in kindergarten, and leaping to 67 percent in grades 1 and 2 combined.
3. In interviews, 45 percent of the preschool teachers reported teaching phonics, contrasting with 80 percent of them who were actually observed teaching phonics (mostly in a contextual

setting); kindergarten teachers, 100 percent; grades 1 and 2 teachers, 96 percent.

4. In contrast to the past research on the inferior effectiveness of teaching phonics (and reading in general) through worksheets and similar isolated learning experiences, 34 percent of the preschool teachers were using them; 75 percent of the kindergarten teachers were; and 81 percent of the grades 1 and 2 teachers were.
5. It seems obvious (to the researchers) that teachers need to be more aware of the various strategies of teaching phonics and select only those strategies that provide students with a positive learning experience.
6. Because only 10 percent of the teachers used a combined approach, most teachers need to learn how to spend more instructional time providing combined phonics and contextual reading experiences.
7. Researchers need to spend more time determining the specific effects of explicit, contextual, and combined phonics teaching strategies on reader and teacher success, and "to determine which strategies are best" (p. 651).

A Review on the Usefulness of Phonics

Groff, P. (1986). The maturing of phonics instruction. *The Reading Teacher, 39,* 919–923.

Conclusions

1. When a spelling pattern doesn't perfectly predict a word's sound, it often provides enough of a clue to enable the reader, with an assist from the author's context, to pronounce the word correctly.
2. The "laborious research to determine which phonics rules had 75 percent utility, and thus deserved to be taught, was beside the point. The waste of time involved (in memorizing the rules) detracts from that available for reading itself" (p. 921).
3. Children need to be pretested on the pronunciation of [spelling patterns], rather than simply be taught the next phonics lesson in the workbook or teacher's manual. Without pretesting students on phonic concepts, unnecessary lessons can steal time from actual reading practice.

4. Teachers need to use a combination of explicit and implicit phonics instruction. The phonogram and vowel pattern methods use both. With highly competent teachers, the analytic and synthetic methods can serve as complementary procedures to each other and to the phonogram and vowel pattern methods.

A Study of What First Graders Tell Us about Phonograms

Wylie, R. E., and Durrell, D. D. (1970). *The Reading Teacher, 39,* 919–923.

Conclusions of Their Study of 900 First Graders

1. It is easier for students to identify phonograms than isolated vowels, e.g., in *cape* or *cap* the **ape** or **ap** rather than just the **a.**
2. Long-vowel phonograms (e.g., **ane, ine, ope**) are just as easy to learn to recognize as short-vowel phonograms (e.g., **ap, op, ug**).
3. Long-vowel phonograms with "silent e" (**ame, ope, ide**) are just as easy to learn to recognize as long-vowel phonograms with vowel digraphs (**ail, eat, oat**).
4. Phonograms containing vowel sounds that are neither long or short (**ark, ool, ound**) can be learned almost as easily and at the same time as phonograms with definite long or short vowels.
5. Phonograms that generate five or more words are almost as easy to learn as phonograms that generate ten or more words. Much of this depends on the meaningfulness of each word to each student.
6. Short-vowel phonograms ending with a single consonant (**an, in, um**) are slightly easier to learn than short-vowel phonograms ending with a consonant digraph (**and, int, ump**).

A Study of the Predictive Power of Vowel Patterns

May, F. B. (1998). How predictive are the vowel patterns? *Reading as Communication, 5th Ed.* Upper Saddle River, NJ: Prentice-Hall.

Discussion. The purpose of this study was to determine how well the five major vowel patterns can predict the correct pronunciation of the vowel sounds. The 1,000 most frequently used words in the English language were examined for that purpose, using a "tough" criterion that required that all words be spelled in such a way that the reader could predict the vowel to be clearly either long or short and not somewhere in between. Consequently, words like *love, gone,* and *practice* were not considered to be sufficiently predictive of the VCE pattern. Because of such limitations, the results were considered to be conservative estimates.

Results and Conclusions

1. The predictive power of the VC pattern (*rip*) was a conservative 86%;
2. The predictive power of the VCC pattern (*risk*) a conservative 89%;
3. The predictive power of the VCE pattern (*ripe*) a conservative 81%;
4. The predictive power of the VVC pattern (*ai, ea, ee, oa*) a conservative 77%;
5. The predictive power of the CV pattern (*go, she, try*) a conservative 77%;
6. The predictive power of vowel patterns appears to be higher than the predictive power of most vowel rules;
7. Spelling patterns appear to be easier for students to remember and use than most vowel rules.

The Adams Research Review on Phonograms

Adams, M. J. (1990). *Beginning to read: Thinking and learning about print.* Cambridge, MA: MIT Press.

Conclusions

1. "As coherent psychological units in themselves, the onset and rime are relatively easy to remember and to splice back together" (p. 324)
2. "They provide a means of introducing and exercising many printed words with relative efficiency, and this is in marked contrast to the slowness with which words can be developed through individual letter–sound correspondences" (p. 324).

3. "Both adults and young children recognize one-syllable words most readily when the words are separated between onsets and rimes" (p. 319).
4. Research has not demonstrated that we should teach phonics in a tight, hierarchical sequence. "The hierarchical model of reading appears to be psychologically faulty. In the reading situations, as in any effective communication situation, the message or text provides but one of the critical sources of information. The rest must come from the readers' own prior knowledge. That knowledge does not function hierarchically from the bottom up but meets the printed information from all levels at once, interactively and in parallel" (p. 291). In short, let the methods of teaching phonics be those that allow for integrating all four cueing systems: graphophonic patterns, sentence structures, contextual word meanings, and the reader's prior knowledge.

A Study of the Limitations of Analogies Based on Phonograms

Bruck, M., and Treiman, R. (1992). Learning to pronounce words: The limitations of analogies. *Reading Research Quarterly 27*, 4, 375–387.

Conclusions

1. "Children use the analogy strategy spontaneously, without explicit [teaching]" (p. 375).
2. "These findings suggest that young children use their knowledge of the rimes of known words to help them pronounce unfamiliar words" (p. 376).
3. Students are more quickly successful in using phonograms to decode words if they have already learned a large number of phoneme–grapheme connections, e.g., *bat* (the unknown word) equals the blend of the separate phonemes /b/ + /a/ + /t/, just as *hat* equals the blend of the known word *hat:* /h/ + /a/ + /t/.

Discussion. I agree with the analytical view presented by Bruck and Treiman in their third conclusion. However, from the instructional viewpoint, phonograms are not learned as isolated phonemes and graphemes. They are learned as simple rimes that are paired with simple onsets, e.g., /c/ + /**ap** / = *cap.* Thus, a great variety of graphemic onsets, like *c* in *cat, ch* in *chest;* or *cl* in *clap,* are learned and pronounced by pairing them with a rime (phonogram). This is a major contrast to attempting to pronounce one phoneme at a time, as in the four-phoneme word, *chest,* /ch/ + /e/ + /s/ + /t/. *Chest* is much easier to recognize as /ch/ + /est/, the much simpler blending of onset and rime.

> The learning of the phonogram **est** provides the student with an immediate awareness of the correct sound required by the short vowel letter, **e.** In short, phoneme–grapheme connections can be learned functionally in the process of creating, repeat reading, writing, and using a list of family words like *best, chest, nest, pest, rest,* and so on.

How are they used? In reading and writing stories both together and individually. If this has not been enough for some students, I have found it advisable to build on the base of phonogram–phonics and develop mastery through synthetic and/or analytic phonics activities.

Myth 3, Part C: A Case Study

At the time I was asked to help Eric, a third grader, he had already been placed in a Title One remedial program. Eric had been in three schools in the past three years, and yet it was reported to me that he had handled each move like a pro. As I began to work with Eric, I was impressed with his drive to learn. He was bright, cheerful, and quite willing to try again and again "until I get it right."

To put it another way, he did not lack for motivation. It was also reported to me that what he did lack was a history of working with teachers who had enough time to tutor him. Consequently, he had learned too little about using the author's context, and almost nothing about relating his reading to the rich background experiences he had accumulated during his nomadic life.

The real kicker was this: He had been taught to read word by word, and to "sound out" every letter of every word. That was his one and only reading strategy. His attitude toward reading was verbalized in this way: "I love to have other people read to me. I don't read very well, but I try to sound out all the words like I'm supposed to."

Samples of Eric's Reading Strategies

Let me show you some samples of how that kind of teaching impeded his progress. I'm going to show you the kinds of errors he made that he never would have made if he had been taught phonics at first with the phonogram method. Here are several sentences he read in a variety of stories. All phonograms suggested are those that can generate ten or more easy words. Next to each sentence, I have indicated how the phonogram method would have saved him from frustration and such extraordinarily slow progress. (Bracketed words are those words not correctly decoded within 5 to 7 seconds. The phonograms are those not recognized by the student.)

1. The trees look /sss-muh/ [*small*].
   Phonogram: **all** in *hall, ball, small, tall.*
2. Plant spiders live in /n/ + /ee/ + /s/ + /t/ + /s/ [*nests*].
   Phonogram: **est** in *best, chest, nest.*
3. Midnight is a black /bl/ [*black*] horse.
   Phonogram: **ack** in *back, black, crack.*
4. And (aw ahh) [*away*] went the bus.
   Phonogram: **ay** in *May, day, way, play.*
5. This black and green one is /cuh/ [*called*] a /pluh/ [*plant*] spider.
   Phonograms: (1) **all** in *ball, call, fall.* (2) **ant** in *pant, plant, slant.*
6. Jack and his /fa fa fa/ [*father*] got on the airplane.
   Phonogram: **ath** as in *bath, math, path* (context cues would provide correct pronunciation; see research by Groff in Part B).
7. We are up /huh/ [high]. (Difficult to decode by sounding out.)
   Phonogram: **ight** in *right, fight, night, sight, light, tight, might,* etc. (context cues needed, as well as mastery of the **ight** phonogram and awareness of the core phonogram **igh** as in *high* and *sigh*).

Observations Related to Eric's Miscues

You have probably already noticed that with miscues 1 through 4 (*small, black, nest, away*) it would have been easy for Eric to use the phonogram method. In #5, Eric would have had a little more difficult task: to pull *call* out of *called,* while at the same time recognizing the phonogram, **all.** In #6, Eric would have had to do what average readers do all the time, according to research on the use of phonics (See Part B). He would have had to use context cues to realize that **ath** in *father* is not pronounced exactly like **ath** in *path, bath, math* or *rather.* However, Groff's research in Part B will show you that most readers can use the combination of **ath** and the author's context to decode *father.*

In #7 (*high*), he would have needed to be somewhat of an expert in using the phonogram method. His background knowledge needed to have included several experiences with the **ight** phonogram, as in *night, right,* and *fight,* and, even better, the uncommon **igh** phonogram, as in *high, sigh,* and *thigh.* He also would have needed a number of experiences in using context cues, which demonstrates an important teaching idea:

> Phonics cues are often useless unless combined with context cues.

In Part E you'll be shown or reminded of how easy it is to teach the phonogram method, using "family word lists," rhyming games, and simple analogies. By this time it was fairly easy to teach this strategy to Eric. With a good deal of guided application of the strategy to his favorite books, his teacher helped him gradually switch from "sounding out every letter" to a phonogram (rime) strategy:

> (1) Search for a well-known rime in the word, and (2) trade the onset of your known word for the onset of the new word. For example, if you already know *mine,* and the new word is *shine,* trade in your /m/ for the /sh/.

By the way, Eric's progress was enhanced even further by catching him up on his "phonemic awareness" (see Chapter 4 on this topic).

Myth 3, Part D: Quick Assessment Techniques for Determining if the Teacher or Student Is Using Strategies Based on the Third Myth of Reading

The following are observation and appraisal instruments for determining the extent to which the teacher and student have "fallen for" the third myth.

Self-Check List for Teacher on Phonics Instruction
Date ________

______ 1. Almost always relies on a teacher's manual for phonics methods.

______ **2.** Relies more on worksheets than books for students' practice.

______ **3.** Depends primarily on phonics worksheets for developing students' mastery of graphophonic letter–sound patterns (or phonics rules).

______ **4.** Has students learn phonics rules rather than visual spelling patterns, for example, VCE (*ice*) or VCC (*ink*) to read and pronounce words correctly.

______ **5.** Teaches students to learn phonics and word recognition basically more through the auditory mode rather than the visual mode.

______ **6.** Feels the synthetic method is good for all students because they learn to make each letter–sound and then blend them together into words.

______ **7.** Advises students to "sound out" words they don't recognize.

______ **8.** Thinks that phonics means "sounding out the words."

______ **9.** Feels that truly professional teachers should use only the phonics method or methods required by the school district.

______ **10.** Often can't recognize high-frequency phonograms in words.

______ **11.** Does not teach students to look for onsets and rimes.

______ **12.** Forgets that onsets can be single letters or digraphs or blends.

______ **13.** Confuses "rhyming words" with "rimes" (phonograms).

______ **14.** Does not readily recognize the five main vowel patterns.

______ **15.** Does not know how to use vowel pattern frames to enable students to learn phonograms and vowel patterns at the same time.

______ **16.** Feels it is not that important for students to enjoy using phonics to help them decode and comprehend an author's message.

______ **17.** Thinks that *heat, Pete,* and *feet* are rhyming words that have the same rime or phonogram.

______ **18.** Usually teaches phonics clues and context clues separately.

______ **19.** Cannot tell the specific differences among the five main phonics teaching methods regarding how they are taught and learned.

______ **20.** Is not well aware of the advantages and disadvantages of each phonics method.

______ **21.** Does not know how to combine the auditory mode with the visual mode of phonics learning.

Symptom Check List for Student: ____________________ Date ________

______ **1.** Perceives phonics as a separate subject in school.

______ **2.** Does not relate phonic worksheets to learning how to read whole texts.

______ **3.** Does not show transfer of phonics lessons to reading of whole text.

______ **4.** Relies on phonics rules but mixes them up.

______ **5.** Has trouble differentiating the sounds of short *i* and short *e;* or the meanings of "short vowel" and "long vowel."

______ **6.** Has trouble blending isolated phonemes into a meaningful word.

______ **7.** Tries to sound out each word, even when a word is already a known sight word.

______ **8.** Perceives reading as a process of "sounding out words."

______ **9.** Doesn't like "to learn phonics."

______ **10.** Seldom recognizes high-frequency phonograms in unknown words.

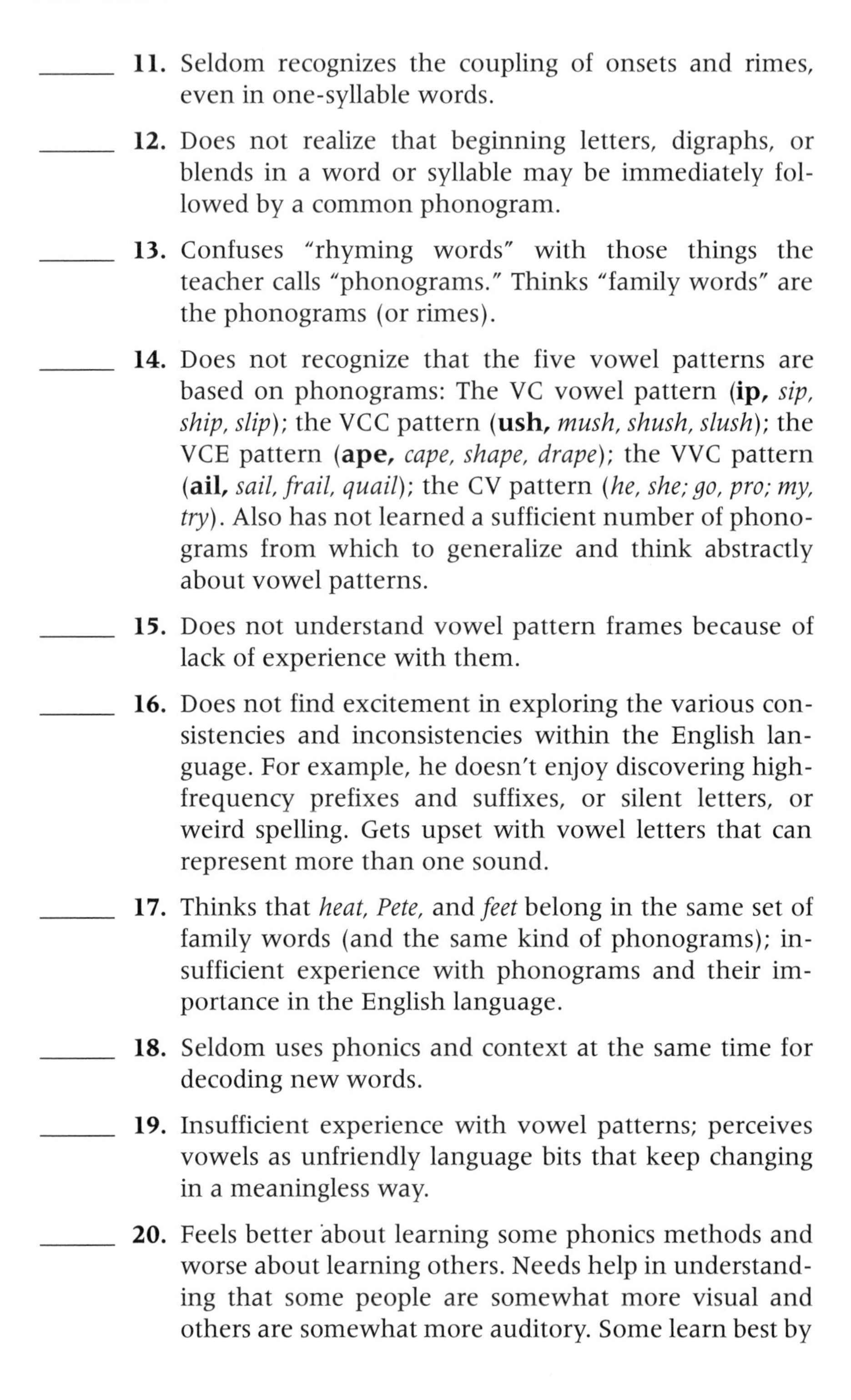

______ **11.** Seldom recognizes the coupling of onsets and rimes, even in one-syllable words.

______ **12.** Does not realize that beginning letters, digraphs, or blends in a word or syllable may be immediately followed by a common phonogram.

______ **13.** Confuses "rhyming words" with those things the teacher calls "phonograms." Thinks "family words" are the phonograms (or rimes).

______ **14.** Does not recognize that the five vowel patterns are based on phonograms: The VC vowel pattern (**ip,** *sip, ship, slip*); the VCC pattern (**ush,** *mush, shush, slush*); the VCE pattern (**ape,** *cape, shape, drape*); the VVC pattern (**ail,** *sail, frail, quail*); the CV pattern (*he, she; go, pro; my, try*). Also has not learned a sufficient number of phonograms from which to generalize and think abstractly about vowel patterns.

______ **15.** Does not understand vowel pattern frames because of lack of experience with them.

______ **16.** Does not find excitement in exploring the various consistencies and inconsistencies within the English language. For example, he doesn't enjoy discovering high-frequency prefixes and suffixes, or silent letters, or weird spelling. Gets upset with vowel letters that can represent more than one sound.

______ **17.** Thinks that *heat, Pete,* and *feet* belong in the same set of family words (and the same kind of phonograms); insufficient experience with phonograms and their importance in the English language.

______ **18.** Seldom uses phonics and context at the same time for decoding new words.

______ **19.** Insufficient experience with vowel patterns; perceives vowels as unfriendly language bits that keep changing in a meaningless way.

______ **20.** Feels better about learning some phonics methods and worse about learning others. Needs help in understanding that some people are somewhat more visual and others are somewhat more auditory. Some learn best by hearing; some by seeing; some by touching; some by moving their body; and most by a combination of two or more ways.

______ **21.** Hasn't learned how to try different phonics strategies; sticks to the one he's used to; needs a more playful way of learning.

The Baf Phonics Test

The Baf Phonics Test can help you determine the exact grapheme–phoneme correspondences the student already has mastered, and it can provide you with a guide to which correspondences the student needs to master as well (see Appendix B).

The Rime Phonics Test

The Rime Phonics Test will help you determine the phonograms your student has already mastered. It will provide you with a guide to which phonograms the student needs to master (see Appendix B).

Myth 3, Part E: Positive Intervention Procedures Designed to Help Overcome the Effects of the Belief that All Phonics Methods Are Equal

An Approximate Sequence for Developing Phonics Mastery

Now I'm going to stick my neck way out (right under the academic guillotine) and provide you with a rough sequence for teaching phonics. This sequence, or a similar sequence, has been used successfully by myself and many of the teachers I have trained for the past twenty years. I don't pretend that this sequence has been tested in a formal research project. It has been tested by each teacher and myself in a way that seemed to evolve and suit the different individuals and groups that we taught. (The learning activities and the order of steps should be modified to match your students' needs and your own needs.)

Step One: Playfully develop their phonemic awareness: Ages 1–5, also children and adults who are learning English as their second language (as demonstrated in Chapter 4).

Without this first step of oral language awareness, students often have difficulty learning phonics (and learning to read). Among the many learning activities for your students, it may help you to include the following:

1. Read rhyming books to them; orally make up short verses together; sing rhyming songs together.
2. Orally and directly develop the more difficult skills of segmenting and blending phonemes (as demonstrated in Chapter 4 and also in *The Phonological Awareness Handbook for Kindergarten and Primary Teachers* by Lita Ericson and Moira Fraser Juliebo, available from the International Reading Association, 800 Barksdale Road, P.O. Box 8139, Newark, Delaware 19714–8139, or www.reading.org).

Step Two: Thoroughly assess students' phonemic awareness. Ages 5–6, or those having trouble learning to read, and ESL children or adults (as shown in Chapter 4 with the *Phonemic Awareness Inventory, PAI, FBM,* 2001). Apply remedial instruction only when necessary, of course, to avoid having them all go through simple phonemic awareness lessons they may no longer need.

Step Three: Teach the oral and written alphabet to mastery. Ages 5–7 and ESL children and adults. This may be the only way you'll be able to adequately communicate with students about phonics and spelling.

Goals: (1) The student or students can sing the alphabet song; (2) say the alphabet in order; (3) observe and call each letter by name, whether lower or upper-case, whether in order or out of order; (4) write each letter in both lower and upper case; (5) independently write and speak their first and last name, address, city, and state; (6) independently speak, write, and "read" their parents' first and last name; (7) independently speak, write, and "read" their telephone number.

Step Four: Teach them how to match the consonant sounds and their corresponding consonant letters. Ages 5.5–6.5+, older children having trouble learning to read, and ESL children or adults.

Teach a few correspondences at a time, e.g., the three correspondences in the word *b-a-t*. At the same time, have them apply what they've learned with "big books," regular books, songs, games, and other activities shown in Appendix D. At first, use only one sound for each consonant, e.g., for *c* and *g* use the hard sound at first and save the soft variations for later. Use dozens of predictable patterned books to help them learn the correspondences enjoyably. In Appendix D you will find a list of 250 patterned books.

> Make each grapheme–phoneme correspondence clear, meaningful, and pleasurable, making certain that you are teaching and challenging rather than merely testing and judging. This positive learning atmosphere can definitely quicken leaners' intuitive insight into the value of phonics to their reading success.

For example, search together for things in the room that begin with the letter *b*. For each thing found in the room, such as a box of crayons, help each student write the word on the board or butcher paper, then say */buh/ box* together. In this way you can use part of the analytic method by orally categorizing according to the same beginning letter and the same beginning sound of all the things in the room that start with the letter *b*. At the same time, you'll be using part of the synthetic method by isolating, blending, and exaggerating the phoneme /b/.

Step Five, Written Vowel/Rime Correspondences: Ages 6–7, older children having trouble with reading, and ESL children or adults.

Teach them the vowel sounds illustrated by those zestful phonograms that busily breed family words. The phonogram **ain,** for example, leads to the creation of *pain, plain, rain, stain, drain, train, brain, gain, grain, main, chain, slain, and vain* (thirteen words in all, not counting Cousin Bl**ain** who loves to rem**ain** and expl**ain** the terr**ain** in Sp**ain.**)

A Sample Lesson Using the Phonogram Method. Let me give you an example of a mother teaching phonics to her child through the use of onsets and rimes. Let's watch how Mom Jones does it with Delilah Jones, her 6½ year old daughter. Mom has a large piece of paper taped to a cupboard door, and has printed two words in a column. Here's the conversation of Mom Jones and Delilah Jones. Feel free to use this scenario as a model for your own teaching:

MJ: Look at the words I've written, *cap* and *lap.*

DJ: *Cap* and *lap.*

MJ: Does *cap* rhyme with *lap*?

DJ: Uh-huh. They both sound the same—sort of.

MJ: That's right. What two letters do they both end with?

DJ: Ummm.... *ap.*

MJ: Good. Can you think of some other rhyming words that end with **ap**?

DJ: (Looking at the word *cap,* thinking about the cap her brother has, and wondering why she doesn't have one.) Uhh, uhh. I can't, Mom.

MJ: (Writing *nap.*) Well, how about *nap*?

DJ: (Gleaming.) Oh! I get it now!! Put *map* up there, and, and *tap* too.

MJ: (While adding to the list.) Would the word, *slap,* work?

DJ: Yeah!

MJ: (While adding to the list.) What else?

DJ: (Now wanting to show off.) *Flap!* And uhh...*trap*!!

MJ: (While adding two more words). Mmm-hmm. What else, honey?

Well, you don't need to watch the rest of the lesson. After Mom and Delilah finished the list, they "echo-read" the words, with Delilah imitating the way her mother said each word. Then they "choral-read" them together. And finally Delilah read them all by herself. Their final list for the first day is on the left.

First Day

c	ap
l	ap
n	ap
m	ap
t	ap
sl	ap
tr	ap
fl	ap
cl	ap

Second Day

	VC
c	ap
l	ap
n	ap
m	ap
t	ap
sl	ap
tr	ap
fl	ap
cl	ap

The next day Mom reviewed the list with a new chart, shown in the righthand column on page 76. When Delilah asked Mom what V–C meant, she said, "V stands for vowel and C stands for consonant. V–C means that all these words have a vowel followed by a consonant at the end of the word.

> "Do you remember all the vowels I taught you?"
> Delilah spoke flippantly like her dad, "Sure do, Sue!"
> "That's cool," Mom said. "What vowel letter do you see in every single word?"
> "Umm I see *a*."
> "And what sound does *a* have in these words?"
> Delilah wrinkled up her nose. "Aahh. It says aahh!" (as in *cat*).

Step Six: Nonsense words to help them achieve mastery of the concept of rimes and onsets. Ages 6.5–7.5, older children if necessary, and with advanced ESL children or adults.

Do the above after they have achieved mastery of at least 50 percent of the phonograms with the VC pattern (**ap, op, ed,** etc.). Do the same thing when you move on to phonograms with the VCC pattern (**est, ash, ock,** etc.). Then do the same thing with VCE, VVC, and finally CV (in that order of difficulty). (See the chart on pages 207–208 for the most frequent phonograms.) For example, after they have achieved mastery of thirteen or more VC phonograms, they may be ready to create nonsense phonograms for this pattern. Here's a workable procedure to follow: Co-create the following list in vertical alphabetical order. Use only single-letter onsets at first: *bad, cad, dad, fad, gad, had, jad, kad, lad, mad, nad, pad, rad, sad, tad, vad, wad, yad, zad.*

Have one student at a time stand up and circle just one word that is not a real word, such as **jad* or **nad.* In this way you will lead your students naturally into discussing the meaning of those words they consider to be real words. (By the way, *wad* is a real word all right, but just tell them, "It doesn't belong to the **jad* family. Why? Because, to be in this family, it has to end in **ad,** *and* it has to rhyme with ["sound like"] the other **ad** words.)" A little later, you can append two-letter onsets as in *clad, glad,* and *Brad.*

Step Seven: Begin Formal Instruction and Practice on Vowel Patterns. Ages 7.5–9, and ESL children or adults.

Before you begin formal instruction make sure your students have created and mastered about 50 percent of the phonograms that will serve as examples for each of the first three out of five vowel patterns: *VC, VCC, VCE, VVC, CV.* (See the chart on page 208.)

The VC short vowel pattern, for instance, fits twenty-six of those famous phonograms that can generate ten or more family words. Your students should have gradually mastered about half, or thirteen, of those phonograms through the use of thirteen different phonogram columns created by you and your students. The columns should have been placed in a VC pattern T-frame, as discussed earlier in Chapter 3, with onsets on the left side of the T, rimes on the right side, and VC on top of the T on the right side. In that way the students would have already become familiar with the concept of a VC pattern such as **at-***cat-scat,* **it-***sit-slit,* and **op-***top-stop.*

Once such mastery has been accomplished with your students, they're ready to stop relying on the crutch you gave them, the vowel pattern frames. Now they're ready to search for VC patterns in the books you're sharing. (At this moment I'm looking at the previous paragraph in this book, and counting the number of words in the first sentence that happen to contain VC phonograms: *p***at***tern,* **in***st***an***ce, f***it***s, phonogr***ams***, c***an,** G**en***erate, t***en,** and *f***am***ily.* That's eight words out of the twenty-one words in the first sentence, almost 40 percent that contain one or more VC short vowel sounds: **at, in, an, it, am, an, en, en, am,** in that order.)

Using Short Stories to Teach Vowel Patterns

What we did with the VC pattern, you can gradually do with the VCC, VCE, VVC, and CV patterns. For some of the patterns you may wish to use something like the following stories, or adapt them to your own students.

The VCE Vowel Pattern: An Ape Tale

Once upon a **time,** there was an **ape** by the **name** of **Kate.** She had a pretty **pale face** that **made** her **mate** feel just **fine.** He **liked** to **take Kate** to a **place** where he could show her off and tell other **apes,** "She's **mine.** But **Kate** was very shy. She would **hide** behind her **mate.** Or she would **ride** away on her **bike.** But **sometimes Kate** would swing with her **mate** on a **rope** or a **vine.** Then her **mate** knew he would **like** her forever.

The VCC Vowel Pattern: A Tale of Jock and Spock

There once was a **sock** whose name was **Jock.**
He went everywhere with his **sock** friend named **Spock.**
They went to **camp** without a **lamp**
And almost **sank** in the river **bank.**

Now they were dirty and **damp.**
And **Spock** got a terrible **cramp** (in his toe).
Jock got a hole and did sink
Right into the water, **kerplink.**

But from his heel floated **lint,**
And this gave the **sock** a big **hint.**
J**ock** knew that **Spock** would see it,
And do his very **best.**

He'd pull him out of the river,
By **long** loose threads on his **chest.**
Yes, **Spock** did **lift** him **quick,** (and said,)
"My friend and I are **thick!**"

Moving on to Instructive Games for Teaching Phonics

Once you have taught leaners the first three patterns, you're ready to have them play certain table games that will solidify their skill in recognizing those three patterns in both short and long words. (See Appendix D for the rules and the simple equipment needed.) As you probably already know, games have proven their worth in teaching sight words, phonograms, vowel patterns, and other letter patterns. Here are some general suggestions for getting the greatest effect from one of those games in Appendix D.

1. The game that I call "Wild Things" has been a favorite among literally thousands of children and adults. It has been very effective in teaching students to recognize both phonograms and vowel patterns. You may duplicate it without permission for your teaching purposes.

2. To get the greatest effect with "Wild Things," you will need to follow the directions very carefully, keeping in mind that this is not only an enjoyable game but also a powerful learning game.

3. It is important that you introduce the game with only two different vowel patterns, preferably the VC pattern (*lap*) and the VCC pattern (*lamp*). After they have come close to mastering those two patterns through the "Wild Things" game, insert a third pattern, VCE (*cape*), into the game. Later, increase the challenge with a fourth pattern, VVC (*leap*). Finally insert the fifth pattern, CV (*she, go, fly*).

4. This means that you will introduce the game with only twenty-five cards: ten VC cards, ten VCC cards, and five "Wild Thing" cards. Then you will increase it to thirty-six cards: ten VC, ten VCC, ten VCE, and six "Wild Thing" cards. Then increase it to forty-seven cards: ten VC, ten VCC, ten VCE, ten VVC cards, and seven "Wild Thing" cards. Finally increase it to fifty-eight cards: ten VC, ten VCC, ten VCE, ten VVC, ten CV and eight "Wild Thing" cards.

5. See Appendix C for your "Source of Words for Each Vowel Pattern."

6. See Appendix D for several other games for teaching phonograms and vowel patterns.

A Quick Summary of Seven Steps Suggested for Phonics Instruction

> Each stage should be mastered, both in isolation and in the context of complete words and messages with equal intensity.

Stage One, Phonemic Awareness: Ages 1–5 (or older if necessary) and ESL children and adults.

Stage Two, Oral Alphabet: Ages 4–5 (or older if necessary) and ESL children or adults.

Stage Three, Written Alphabet: Ages 5–6 (or older if necessary) and ESL children and adults.

Stage Four, Real Phonics Begins: Ages 5.5–6.5 + (or older if necessary) and ESL children and adults.

Stage Five, Written Vowel/Rime Correspondences: Ages 6–7 (or older if necessary) and ESL children and adults.

Stage Six, Nonsense Words: Ages 6.5–8 (or older if necessary) and ESL children and adults.

Stage Seven, Begin Formal Instruction and Practice on Vowel Patterns. Ages 7–9 (or older if necessary) and ESL children and adults.

Overall Implications for Positive Intervention in Teaching Phonics

Implication 1: Starting with Step 4 (Real Phonics Begins), it would be advisable to supplement (but not supplant) the phonogram–vowel pattern methods with one or more highly specific advantages of the synthetic method.

1. Having your students write the letters and words makes it easier for them to recognize those letters and words in the future.
2. Having students attempt to make the sound of isolated phonemes can help many students recognize the correspondence between letters and sounds. (This does not imply that the learning of initial phonograms, e.g., **ca** in *cape* is as helpful and meaningful as using final phonograms, e.g., **ape** in *cape.*)

Implication 2: Beginning with Step 4 (Real Phonics Begins), it would be advisable to supplement (but not supplant) the phonogram–vowel pattern methods with one or more highly specific advantages of the analytic method.

1. It is usually helpful to students to notice the correspondence between a phoneme (such as the sound /ch/) and its representative grapheme (such as the digraph **ch**) in the natural linguistic context of whole words, sentences, and stories. This does not mean that words and phonemes always have to be examined in context. Phonics instruction need not be an either–or procedure.
2. Both the analytic and phonogram methods can provide opportunities for students to learn through an observation and discovery approach. Such an approach is at least conducive to expanding their abilities to think in the following ways:
   a. Creating and using categories of information;
   b. Using constructivist thinking processes to produce their own knowledge;
   c. Believing in their own power to learn on their own or in collaboration with others.

Implication 3: There are times when your teaching methods are less important than your concepts of learning. For instance, you will find in Chapter 4 that studies of phonemic awareness indicate that learning how to segment words into their onsets and rimes, e.g., *place* = **pl** + **ace,** is not enough. The intuitive realization that spoken words are made up of phonemes is a concept of equal or even greater importance.

Implication 4: Let me urge you to move on to Chapter 4 for purposes of refining your knowledge of phonological awareness in general and phonemic awareness in particular. These are crucial forms of awareness with respect to learning and teaching phonics.

A Summary of Chapter 3

1. Phonic methods are definitely not equal. Nor is any one method appropriate for every student. But the phonogram–phonics method seems to have the greatest potential for an appropriate beginning method of teaching phonics.

2. However, all phonics methods, including even the phonogram–phonics method can be more effective when preceded by intensive phonological awareness training. (The most efficient time for this training is in kindergarten and, even earlier, in informal settings such as the home.)

3. Teaching the recognition of rimes and onsets is an effective way of helping children build confidence in their ability to analyze and pronounce both one-syllable words and multisyllabic words.

4. The learning of rimes and onsets can lead gradually to the mastery of four common vowel patterns: VC (*at, hat*), VCC (*ant, pant*), VCE (*ate, hate*), VVC (*eat, heat*). The use of phonograms (rimes) and vowel patterns can increase reading fluency and comprehension.

5. After teaching the phonogram–phonics method, you can follow up with synthetic phonics activities, especially for students who need more practice on auditory recognition and memory of phonemic patterns.

6. After teaching the phonogram–phonics method, you can also follow up with analytic phonics activities, especially for students who need more practice on visual recognition and memory of grapheme patterns.

7. This chapter provides you with a seven-step program for learning phonics that seems to work well for most students. These stages generally begin in preschool, and some of them continue throughout the study of the English language. (A caveat: Students continue throughout schooling to be variable [to the nth degree] in their learning pace, abilities, and styles.)

> Each phonics method has disadvantages that may need to be compensated for through the use of one or more of the other phonics methods. Compensation is the name of the game when teaching reading. Making one favorite phonics method your "fits all" approach is simply not fair to your "clients."

CHAPTER

4 The Fourth Myth of Reading

Myth 4, Part A: Phonological Awareness Training Is Not Necessary, because reading novices get the same thing from early phonics training.

The Difference between Phonics and Phonological Awareness

Do you have a student who has trouble distinguishing one phonogram or vowel pattern from another? Some of my students, for example, have read a spelling pattern like c-a-n-e as *can,* or a pattern like p-a-d as *paid.* This, of course, is just one example of a phonics problem (or, more precisely, a graphophonics problem). Problems like this are the kind you're probably already capable of solving, in collaboration with your students. (See Chapter 3 if I'm wrong about that.)

> *"Phonics"* (graphophonics) refers to a process of matching phonemes and phoneme patterns with graphemes and grapheme patterns (sound patterns with letter patterns).

If That's Phonics, Then What Is Phonological Awareness All about?

Sometimes we think students have a phonics problem, when actually they have a phonological awareness problem. Let's imagine that you're reading the following questions to a student. (But you're not writing anything for him or her to read. You want good listening instead.) How well do you think this student would do on these questions (selected from the *Phonological Awareness Interview.*)

1. What happens to the sound, /at/. If you make this little sound [breathy] fff right before **at**? What word do you get?
2. Try the sound /zzz/ just before **at**. Did you get a real word or a silly word? Say it for me, please.
3. I'll take apart the little sounds in the word, and you put the sounds back together again: /f/.../a/.../n/. What word am I thinking of?
4. Let's play a guessing game: I'm thinking of three words. The first word is /p/-/p/-/p/-/p/-/paper/. What's the word?
5. Now that you guessed that word, make up the next word, yourself, a word that starts with /b/-/b/-/b/-/b/.
6. O. K., now tell me a short word that starts with /duh/. [lightly] Now give me a longer word that starts with /duh/, a word that has two big sounds like *danger* [dane!—jer!].
7. Listen to the three little sounds in every word. Find the word with one little sound that isn't the same as the other three words have.

   pin, pig, dog, leg [repeat] Why? [/g/ versus /n/]
8. How many little sounds in Jack? What are those little sounds?
9. Give me three real words, or silly words, that rhyme with *bad, mad, zad,* and *blad.*
10. Let's play a game called "Steal the Sound." What is the second little sound in *blad*? If we take that sound away, what word do you have left?

> As you can see from studying those ten examples, "phonological awareness" is different from phonics (graphophonics). Phonological awareness includes students' ability to hear and recognize phonemes, syllables, rhymes, alliteration, and other forms of oral language.

But What Is "Phonemic Awareness" All about?

Phonological awareness relies mostly on phonemic awareness, which includes several abilities crucial for spelling and reading. The learner must:

1. Segment (separate) a word into its phonemes by estimating the sound of each phoneme in the word. Example: The spoken word, *bled,* can be segmented into the sounds, /b/ + /l/ +/e/ + /d/.
2. Blend each phoneme orally into a real word. Example: The sound of each phoneme, /b/ + /l/ +/e/ + /d/ can be blended into the spoken word *bled.*

3. Insert a single phoneme into a word. Example: The phoneme /n/ can be inserted into the spoken word *bled* to get *blend.*
4. Remove a single phoneme from a word. Example: The phoneme /l/ can be removed from *bled* to get *bed.*

Phonemic awareness is at the core of phonological awareness, because it requires a student's ability to hear and recognize the differences among the various phonemes within a word. For instance, your student, call her Manora, must notice that the spoken word *shop* is made up of three sequential language sounds: /sh/ + /o/ +/p/. Without at least a semiconscious awareness of phonemes, she may have great difficulty later in determining how to write a word like *shop* that she has never had the need to write before.

Likewise, she may have great difficulty in independently reading a word like shop that she has never had to read before. To understand this better, think of a strange one-syllable word like **jad.* Notice how you have to estimate the separate sounds of /j/ + /a/ + /d/ as you write the three letters that represent those sounds: j + a + d.

Does Phonemic Awareness Assist in Recognizing Onsets and Rimes?

Even the ability to recognize rhyming words with their onsets and rimes (phonograms) is based partially on phonemic awareness. For instance the student has to recognize in *had* and *bad* the sound, /ad/, which in turn is made up of the phonemes /a/ and /d/ (whether we consciously realize this or not). The student also has to hear and recognize the difference between the phoneme /h/ in *had* and the phoneme /b/ in *bad.*

> Without phoneme awareness we would be without our most important ally in the endeavor to become literate (both in reading and writing).

The Necessity of Phonemic Awareness to the Ability to Read

A considerable amount of research, which you can read about in Part B of this chapter, demonstrates that learners with a low level of phonemic awareness very often have difficulty in becoming competent readers of the English language. For example, several researchers have found that dyslexic and at-risk readers usually do poorly on measures of phonemic awareness.

Exacerbating the Problem of a Low Level of Phonemic Awareness

In spite of our good intentions, we teachers (and parents) often handle the reading problems of poor readers by magnifying the problem. If a student is not doing well "with phonics," we frequently provide or demand more and more phonics training.

Does it work? To a very limited extent it does help them build their sight vocabulary (and consequently, their comprehension). The side effects, though, are not so good, because these readers are now imprisoned by their own sight vocabulary, restrained from independently reading and writing new words that are not yet part of their memory bank.

Why is this true? Probably because they have not been made aware of the differences among phonemes. For instance, they can't listen to a new word like *drag* and quickly segment it into the sounds, /d/ + /r/ + /a/ + /g/. Consequently it is difficult for them to independently spell the word, *drag,* without rummaging through their stock of sight words. Frantically, their brain searches for graphically and phonemically similar sight words stored in its memory, familiar words like *door, dig, drum,* or *drug.*

What's worse, it's equally difficult for them to read the new word, *drag,* without relying on sight words similar in graphemes and phonemes. Of course, if your students are advanced in their visual memory, they might be able to recognize the last two letters as the phonogram, **ag,** and come up with a memory of a word like *bag,* which, through the analogy process could possibly lead to *drag.*

The Most Important Point: Phonemic Awareness before Phonics

Those of us who assist students in learning to read can be a bit naïve when we try to help them by simply providing an ever-increasing pile of phonics worksheets or workbooks. By now it may be obvious to you that this treatment of our children and our second language adults is putting Treatment B (phonics) before Treatment A (phonemic awareness). The Early Phonics Programs, that some of our state and federal Departments of Education are insisting on (with good intentions) are putting the abstract, written form of language before the inceptive spoken language. Consequently, we are most likely increasing the number of students with severe reading problems.

I hope you don't feel as guilty as I still do about similar mistakes in my past. But do consider this: If you and I were treated by a doctor with Treatment B before the all important, preparatory Treatment A, would we laughingly consider the doctor "naïve," or would we angrily consider that doctor incompetent and subject to a suit? (It gives me the chills.)

Temptations to Rely on Synthetic Phonics over Phonemic Awareness

In the past, and moving right up to the present, one of the solutions to this problem has been the use of the synthetic method of teaching phonics, described in Chapter 3. This method requires the student to perceive letters not as symbols of sounds but as the sounds themselves. The letter *s*, for instance, is spoken as sss and students are to blend all of the different "letter sounds" into one word.

The advantages and disadvantages of this method are described in Chapter 3, but the main disadvantages of using this method as your combined phonemic awareness and phonics methods are these:

1. Many learners have not had phonemic awareness experiences, and therefore you'll place them immediately into an unnecessary failure situation For example, the sound of the three-syllable word *banana* becomes, for those without phoneme awareness preparation, a meaningless six-syllable word, /buh-ahh-nuh-ahh-nuh-ahh/.

2. Thus, the students are still dependent on their memory of sight words and, in some cases, on having their teacher walk around the classroom helping them "sound out" words they can't read. In short, the students are not learning how to be independent readers and problem solvers.

3. As you'll see later in Part B, learning phonemic analysis (in a playful way) before attempting to learn phonics, has been shown by researchers to be beneficial in helping learners to read and spell.

The Time and Place for Learning Phonological Awareness

When should learners develop phonological awareness? The best way for the majority of students to become independent readers and spellers is probably to begin at the beginning of language, i.e., orally, at the phonemic awareness level. This means before they are introduced to the much more abstract language of written letters and words. It also means before phonics (graphophonics) is introduced with its requirement of translating graphemes into phonemes (and vice versa for spelling).

Ideally, this introduction to phonemic awareness should occur in the home, long before formal schooling. But you and I both know that "should" is seldom "will." For many children who are not abundantly read to and written to at home, phonemic awareness training does not begin before kindergarten or even first grade. For many others the training does not begin at all. Why? Perhaps because millions of parents and teachers today have not had the opportunity to learn the values of such training for their children, nor have they had such training themselves.

The Importance of Parents' Role in Introducing Phonemic Awareness

Let me hasten to point out that other millions of parents, siblings, and early childhood teachers have indirectly introduced certain aspects of phonological awareness to very young novices. (In one documented case, "reading together" began on the day after birth. See Part B of this chapter.) How? By reading aloud to them or reciting rhymes, jingles, songs, nursery rhymes, and other forms of language. Many of the books by Dr. Seuss are helpful in introducing phonological awareness, particularly the one called *There's a Wocket in My Pocket.* The book by J. Tomkins called *When a Bear Bakes a Cake* is very good for introducing both rhyming and the manipulation of phonemes.

The School's Vital Role in Introducing and Mastering Phonemic Awareness

Those types of indirect teaching do provide children with an excellent start. There are several reasons, though, for the schools to take a key role in helping students master their phonemic awareness of the English language. One reason is the professional skill and knowledge required for teaching phonemic segmenting and blending to novices of different backgrounds and abilities. Another reason for school involvement is the lack of awareness of many parents and other adults as to the crucial difference between phonics training and phonemic training.

A Teaching Problem for All Adults: Child versus Adult Language

We adults seldom remember the differences between our childhood understanding of language and our adult understanding of language. As the years fly by, we become used to "abstracting" (mentally boiling down) our belongings—houses, money, cars, and other valuable items—into the concept of "wealth" or "assets." Finally we abstract (boil down) the oral symbols into the written form of the words *wealth* and *assets* that you are reading right now. We start with a bunch of real things and real experiences, then boil and boil and boil, until we have only those tiny bits of scribbled ink that we call "words."

Such words, and all other words, written or spoken, are nothing more and nothing less than culturally agreed-on symbols of those real things and real experiences. As adults we have learned, for efficiency's sake, to perceive a word as if the word were the actual object or experience. As very young children, though, such adult symbols were magical or nonsensical to us. After all, who in their right mind would insist that the sequential symbols, a-p-p-l-e refer to a real apple?

If you saw the movie, *A New Start,* about a blind man who was able to regain his sight, you might understand very clearly what I'm talking about. That man got his sight back, all right, but now his brain had to learn every important concept that he had missed out on during his blindness. It was extremely hard for his loving girlfriend to understand why he was now having so much trouble relating to someone who had already developed those concepts.

You probably see the analogy I'm making: How difficult it often is for children and non-English speaking adults to perceive the world in the way adults do who have mastered the English language. With respect to language, you have already mastered the challenging process of abstracting things and experiences into words and written symbols. They are just beginning to understand what you have understood for many years. And to put it into clearer perspective yet, you and I have enjoyed the benefit of all those humans over time and space and cultures that have had abundant opportunities to abstract, generalize, stereotype, analyze, and synthesize or, more simply, to "boil down" reality into symbols like words and letters.

This problem of teaching students the symbolic system of reading and spelling is very similar to the problem of teaching arithmetic to them. The adult teacher, like other adults, has been gradually conditioned to perceive the strange squiggle 6 as referring to six real things. The learner, on the other hand, needs something much more concrete than the numeral 6: six apples, six pencils, or at least six X's on the chalkboard. Our student's understanding, in my estimation, requires something ten times more concrete than spoken symbols; and one hundred times more concrete than written symbols.

How Much Time Is Needed for Learning to Perceive Things Abstractly?

The neophyte reader, writer, and "arithmeticker" needs time for many years of experience to learn how to automatically abstract real things into symbolic letters and numerals. Time to boil down her living experiences, her learning experiences, her listening, speaking, and writing experiences, her "being-read-to" experiences, her counting experiences, until she's finally prepared to trust the world's reasons for representing objects and experiences with symbols called letters or numerals. (I have known many adults who are not yet ready to let objects or experiences be represented by symbols. In fact, I wish I had one hundred dollars for every time I have regressed to counting on my fingers.)

The beginning reader of English needs time to hear the phonemes of our language in rhyming words, such as those in the fly fisherman's appeal: "Hi, guy. Try my dry fly"; alliterative words, such as "Larry Lang likes little lazy lambs"; silly words like *bibbity-bobbity-boo,* or *supercalifragilisticespialidotious;* or catchy verses: Pig: *How now, thou brown cow?* Cow: *Bow down, thou foul sow.*

Or one of those "alphabet soups," containing all of the letters in the alphabet: *The quick brown fox jumped over the lazy dog.* Or Big Bird's 10-syllable alphabet song: "ab-cd-ef-ghij-klm-nop-qrst-uv-wx-yz" pronounced something like this: ab-could-eff-gije-klim-nop-krist-yuve-wix-yuz.

> In conclusion, beginning readers need time to play with their language before they have to work with it, time to mix "things" with language and blend "experiences" with even more language. Time to play with phonemes before abstracting them into graphemes (writing). Time to play with even more phonemes before translating other people's graphemes back into phonemes (reading). Time for connecting—back and forth, forth and back—the familiar sounds with the more abstract letters, the familiar with the abstract...ad infinitum.

Myth 4, Part B: Research That Refutes the Fourth Myth of Reading

A Comparison of Intelligence Scores with Phonemic Awareness Scores in Predicting Reading Success

Stanovich, K., Cunningham, A., & Cramer, B. (1984). Assessing phonological awareness in kindergarten children: Issues of task comparability. *Journal of Experimental Child Psychology, 38,* 175–190.

Results

Phonemic awareness scores in kindergarten were better predictors of reading ability, one year later, than intelligence test scores. (Both predictor tests were administered at the same time.)

A Review of Research on the Impact of a High Level of Phonological Awareness on Learning to Read and Spell

Cardoso-Martins, C. (1995). Sensitivity to rhymes, syllables, and phonemes in literacy acquisition [in English and Portuguese]. *Reading Research Quarterly, 30,* 4, 808–828.

Results and Conclusions

1. With languages that have an alphabetic spelling system, phonological awareness can have a major impact on the acquisition of reading and spelling abilities.
2. All researchers on phonological awareness have found high correlations between children's performance on phonemic awareness tasks and their success in learning to read and spell.
3. The recognition of rhyming words probably involves, among other factors, the reader's recognition of identical phonemes in each cluster of rhyming words.

A Developmental Study of Phonological Awareness and Reading

Bryant, P., Maclean, M., Bradley, L., & Crossland, J. (1990). *Developmental Psychology, 26,* 429–438.

Conclusions

1. Experience with rhyming words can increase the sensitivity to phonemes, which later assists the student in understanding grapheme–phoneme correspondences.
2. This, in turn, can assist the student's ability to read by translating graphemes into phonemes (or to write by translating phonemes into graphemes).

Correlations between Early Sensitivity to Rhymes and Later Reading and Spelling

Goswami, U., & Bryant, P. (1992). Rhyme, analogy, and children's reading. In P. Gough, L. Ehri, & R. Treiman (Eds.), *Reading acquisition* (pp. 49–63). Hillsdale, NJ: Erlbaum.

Results

Significant correlations were found between sensitivity to rhyming sounds and later progress in learning to read and spell. Because correlations can be interpreted in many ways, it is more important that the rhyme scores were significantly accurate predictors of students' spelling and reading scores two and three years later.

A Study of the Effects of Phoneme Awareness Training

Ball, E., & Blachman, B. (1991). Does phoneme awareness training in kindergarten make a difference in early word recognition and developmental spelling? *Reading Research Quarterly, 26,* 49–66.

Results and Conclusions

1. A comparison of three randomly assigned groups and treatments demonstrated that direct phoneme segmentation training, combined with letter name instruction and instruction in letter/sound correspondences, was the most effective way to develop word identification skill.
2. Letter-name and letter-sound training, without phoneme awareness training, was not enough to develop word identification skill.
3. Increased letter-sound knowledge, by itself, did not improve the skill of segmenting phonemes. (This is another example of the need for phonemic analysis training before teaching phonics.)

Activities such as merely holding up letter flashcards and asking students to "give me the sound of this letter," do not train students in the segmentation and blending skills so necessary for real reading and real writing.)

4. Phoneme awareness can be effectively gained through direct instruction. (Direct teaching should be augmented by indirect practice through the use of family-word charts, games that employ the separation and junction of onsets and rimes (phonograms), and writing activities that employ alliteration.

> Early reading difficulties, many of them caused by a low level of phoneme awareness, can have long-lasting effects (if there is no intervention) on vocabulary development, concept development, and even syntactic knowledge (not to mention emotional development).

A Study of the Effects of Early Stimulation of Phonological Awareness

Lundberg, I., Frost, J., & Petersen, O. (1988). Effects of an extensive program for stimulating phonological awareness in preschool children. *Reading Research Quarterly, 23,* 263–284.

Results and Conclusions

1. In this tightly controlled, longitudinal study from K through 2, it was found that phonemic awareness can be developed prior to phonics and other literacy instruction, as well as independently of such instruction.
2. The segmentation ability (separation of phonemes within whole words) does not develop spontaneously, but explicit direct instruction in segmentation can have a major impact on learning to read and spell.
3. The segmentation training (exercises and games) of 15 to 20 minutes a day for 8 months had a lasting effect on the children's progress in first and second grade (the total length of the study).

Research to Determine the Best Predictor of Literacy

Nation, K., & Hulme, C. (1997). Phonemic segmentation, not onset-rime segmentation, predicts early reading and spelling skills. *Reading Research Quarterly, 32,* 2, 154–167.

Results and Conclusions

1. Phonemic segmentation ability is a superior predictor of reading and spelling ability, far superior to one's rhyming ability. (Note, however, that the use of onsets and rimes, phonograms, provides additional segmentation training through the automatic comparison of the phonemes in both onsets and rimes.)
2. A measurement of phonemic segmentation ability is probably the most effective device for identifying students who need extensive training toward this vital skill.
3. Phonemic segmentation training may be even more powerful if linked to training in recognizing spelling patterns. (The researchers speculated on this possibility but did not adequately demonstrate the connection. Much more research needs to be done on this kind of combined phonemic awareness and spelling–phonics training. Other research inspires serious doubts whether the combined approach is more effective than starting with phonemic awareness training and leading gradually to phonics. It is probably a mistake to consider the combined approach to be more efficient. In the long run it could be highly inefficient.)
4. Learning to spell is probably even more dependent on phonological skills than learning to read. Consequently, early experiences and training in phonemic awareness can be highly important for both reading and writing achievement.

Once again, I suggest that we move students gradually from concrete to abstract, from familiar to unfamiliar, using flexible variations of the following sequence, noting especially #11.

1. Spontaneous intuitive oral language play (home & school, hereafter h & s)
2. Listening to rhymes and alliteration (school & home, hereafter s & h)
3. Collaborative oral creation of rhymes and alliteration (h & s)
4. Intensive instruction: phoneme segmentation and blending (s)
5. Introduction of phonics through the phonogram approach with rimes and onsets that produce family words (s & h)
6. Modeling of how to connect the phonemes and the corresponding graphemes of onsets and rimes (s)

7. Modeling of how to connect between phonograms and the five consistent vowel patterns (VC, VCC, VCE, VVC, and CV) (s)
8. Modeling the recognition of graphophonic vowel patterns (s)
9. Modeling of how to connect phonemes and the corresponding graphemes of nonrhyming words (s)
10. Using formal synthetic, analytic, or combined phonics methods with students who need additional instruction (s)

11. Giving continuous attention (in #1 through #10) to the collaboration of phonics and meaning (words and messages) (s&h)

Myth 4, Part C: A Case Study Illustrating the Effects of Teaching Phonics without First Teaching Phonological Awareness

Maddy was close to finishing her first-grade school year when I was asked to help her teacher decide whether to hold her back in first grade for another year. As I listened to her reading to me, I was hard put to stay objective. I had just been bludgeoned with the teacher's and mother's oft repeated diagnosis: "She's definitely learning disabled," they kept saying. "Very disabled."

My lack of objectivity came not from my confidence in their assessment, but from my irritation that Mandy had been labeled rather than assessed. The more I listened to her bravely stumble through a below-grade-level primer selection, the sadder I became. It was obvious to me that this child had not been given much of a chance to use her mind and her natural problem-solving abilities. Only with intensive prompting did she attempt to use her own background experiences or the author's context or even the canned introduction that I read to her before she began to read.

It was painfully clear to me, in my biased mind, that she had been taught to read for words and not for messages. Over half of her effort was devoted to using whatever sight words she had memorized in kindergarten and first grade. As a result of my lack of objectivity, I assessed her in a simplistic way as having been "taught to read via the word-by-word method." Here's one of many examples of how she read, but first notice how much background information she was given in the introduction:

This is a story about Jack and his father. They're going to fly on an airplane together. Find out what Jack saw from way up high in the sky.

1. Author: Jack and his father got on the airplane.

   Maddy: Jack and the fat go to his plane.

2. Author: Away they flew.

   Maddy: Away with NS. (NS means a no-show. The teacher had to give her the last word, *flew.*)

3. Author: "We are up high," said Jack.

   Maddy: "We and up in in," sad Jack.

4. Author: "The trees look small."

   Maddy: "They went too small."

5. Author: "And so do the animals," said Father.

   Maddy: "And so do the...avenue,"* sad Fat.

6. Author: Jack said, "This is fun!"

   Maddy: Jack is sad this day.

Some Probable Reasons for Maddy's Reading Difficulties

My first biased observation, you will remember, was that Maddy had been taught to read for words instead of messages. As I studied her recorded miscues, though, I grew less confident. My second observation was that Maddy might have been taught to think very little about the author's context or her own related experiences.

For example, Sentence #1 was interpreted this way: "Jack and the fat go to his plane." This doesn't appear to relate to her own experiences, does it? But it might relate to the sight words Maddy had obviously accumulated: *Jack, and, the, fat, go, to, his, plane.* When I looked at her miscues a second time, though, I realized that, "Jack and the fat go to his plane" could possibly fit her past experiences.

* I was so curious about this substitute of *avenue* for *animals* I asked if she lived on a street or and on an avenue. Her reply was, "I live on Cherry Avenue."

(You see, when I was talking with Maddy's mother, I did notice she was extremely overweight.) And so, Maddy might have been, at least occasionally, trying to make sense out of the author's message.

If Maddy was not necessarily handicapped by a word by word method of reading, then what was her handicap? The answer came unknowingly from her teacher, who told me later that day about Maddy's reported difficulty in kindergarten. "She came to my class without learning a bit of phonics—in spite of all the work her teacher had gone through to prepare them for first grade...you know, with a good phonics background."

Flash! The light went on. All that effort Maddy had made to memorize sight words. And why? Because she hadn't been prepared to grasp phonics, and therefore had no other choice than to rely on sight words. But wait a minute. Exactly why had she not been able to grasp that important tool?

You're right. From what I verified later that day, she had not been prepared for phonics. No assessment of her phonemic awareness had been done. No special training was provided for in the school curriculum plans.

End of story. I turned in my report, offered to provide her and her teacher with phoneme awareness exercises and games, and promised myself to stay out of the assessment rut I had dug for myself.

Myth 4, Part D: Determining the Compensatory Instruction Needed to Overcome the Effects of the Fourth Myth

If you have a student who is having trouble learning and making use of phonics, and thus having trouble reading in general, I would recommend that you informally interview that student to determine whether phonemic awareness has or has not been learned.

In this part of Chapter 4, I have provided you with the type of interview questions that have been useful in determining the approximate level of competence that a student has reached in phonological awareness. You were given a few sample questions in Part A, but in this part you will be able to examine the entire interview and ways of using it. Please note that the questions are not just for assessment but for instruction of those students who need to reach a higher level of phonemic awareness in order to become good readers.

BOX 4.1

Phonological Awareness Interview*

This oral and aural assessment tool, the Phonological Awareness Interview, has been designed for informal observation of strengths and weaknesses in phonemic awareness, rhyme awareness, syllable awareness, word awareness, and alliteration awareness. It can be used as an observation checklist for teachers, a guide for instructional exercises, and a research tool for creating phonological awareness scores. If necessary, the questions asked during the interview may be modified to more closely fit the student or students you are assessing. However, all questions and challenges have been written to be used with ages 5 through 7 and through adulthood.

General Directions for Administration

For the sake of validity and reliability, it is important to pronounce all phonemes in a light breathy way with extremely little vibration of the throat. The phoneme /b/, for instance, should be pronounced without any of the vibration necessary for words like *baby* or *babble*. Words in parentheses are for the interviewer only.

For easy recording, check only answers you consider to be correct. There are exactly 50 items for an interview of approximately 30 minutes. (This amount of time and items should allow for accurate checks on local reliability, local validity, and easy computation of percentages.

For your ease in administration, we have exaggerated or blended some of the sounds, e.g., /at/ for /a/+/t/ or /huh/ for /h/.

Name ______ **Age** ______ **Grade** ______ **Date** ______ **Score %** ______

A sample question: "What happens to the sound, /**at**/, if you put the (breathy) /kuh/ sound right before /**at**/. What word do you get? Yes, you get kuh-at. You get the word *cat.*

_____ **1.** What happens to the sound /**at**/ if you make this little sound (breathy) /fff/ right before /**at**/? What word do you get?

_____ **2.** What happens when you make the sound /**sss**/ before **at?**

_____ **3.** When you make the (breathy) sound, /huh/, before **at?**

_____ **4.** When you make the (breathy) sound, /buh/, before **at?**

_____ **5.** Try the sound /zzz/ just before **at.**

_____ **6.** Did you get a real word or a silly word?

_____ **7.** Try the (breathy) sound /duh/ before **at.**

_____ **8.** Did you get a real word or a silly word?

_____ **9.** Why was it a silly word?

_____ **10.** What is this word? /p/-/p/-/p/-/p/-paper.

_____ **11.** What is this word? /t/-/t/-/t/-/t/-table.

_____ **12.** What is this word? /m/-/m/-/m/-/m/-mother.

_____ **13.** Make up a word that begins with /b/-/b/-/b/-/b/-

_____ **14.** Make up a word that begins with /k/-/k/-/k-/k/-

_____ **15.** Make up a word that begins with /s/-/s/-/s/-/s/-

_____ **16.** What word am I thinking of? I'll break the word into three little sounds. Then you put the sounds together again. The word I'm thinking of has three soft sounds: /f/.../a/.../n/. What word is that?

_____ **17.** Here's the second word: /t/.../o/.../p/. What word is that?

_____ **18.** Here's the third word: /m/.../u/.../d/. What word is that?

_____ **19.** Which of these words is a silly word: *fan, pud,* or *top*? (repeat)

_____ **20.** Why is *pud* a silly word?

_____ **21.** Let me hear you make the first little sound in your first name.

_____ **22.** Let me hear you make the last little sound in your first name.

_____ **23.** Give me a short word that begins with (breathy) /duh/.

_____ **24.** How many little sounds do you hear in that word?

_____ **25.** All right. How many BIG sounds to you hear in *Fri-day*? [2]

_____ **26.** Give me another word with exactly two BIG sounds.

_____ **27.** How many BIG sounds in the word, /buh/ /na/ /nuh/. [3]

_____ **28.** Give me another word with exactly three BIG sounds.

_____ **29.** Give me a word with the sound /aahh/ (short a) in the middle.

(continued)

Continued

___ **30.** How many little sounds do you hear in the word *nap*?

___ **31.** How many BIG sounds do you hear in the word *nap-ping*? [2]

___ **32.** How many little sounds do you hear in *Jack*? [3]

___ **33.** How many BIG sounds do you hear in *Jack*?

___ **34.** How many little sounds in *chips*? [4] What are those sounds?

___ **35.** How many BIG sounds in *robin*? [2] What are those sounds?

___ **36.** How many little sounds in *robin*? [5] What are those sounds?

Listen to the three little sounds in every word. Find the word that does not have the same little sound that the other three words have. Here is a sample: *bun, bad, bet, dig*. Why did you pick *dig*? Here are some more for you to try:

___ **37.** big, ball, bed, kick (repeat). Why? [/b/ versus /k/]

___ **38.** pin, pig, dog, leg (repeat). Why? [/g/ versus /n/]

___ **39.** sip, cap, ball, hop (repeat). Why? [/p/ versus /l/]

___ **40.** fun, fin, run, bun (repeat). Why? [/u/ versus /i/]

___ **41.** Give me two words that rhyme with *had* and *glad* (usual responses include *bad, dad, mad, pad, Brad, lad,* etc.).

___ **42.** Give me one silly word that rhymes with **zad* and **blad*.

Okay, now you're ready to play a game called "Steal the Sound."

___ **43.** What is the second little sound in **blad*? /l/

___ **44.** All right, if I steal that sound away from you, what word do you have left? Go ahead and steal the /l/ sound from *blad*. Instead of **blad* you now have a real word. What word do you have now? [*bad*]

___ **45.** Steal the first sound from **glip*, and what word do you get?

___ **46.** Steal the second sound from **stap;* what word do you get?

____ **47.** Steal the third sound from *fast,* and what do you get?

Now we're going to play a detective game. Are you ready to be a detective? Okay, here's what you have to find. I was going to read you a sentence about a little lobster. But my sentence is missing the last word, and you have to find it. Here are some clues for you: The last word in my sentence must start with the first sound you hear in *little* and *lobster.*

____ **48.** What is the first sound in *little* and in *lobster*?

Okay, now listen to the next clue so you can find the missing word in my sentence. The missing word has the same first sound as *little* and *lobster.* (Repeat directions before each sentence)

a. The little lobster lost his ball. [yes or no]

b. The little lobster lost his sailboat. [yes or no]

c. The little lobster lost his lunch. [yes or no]

____ **49.** Now let's try a sentence about a baby bear. This time you must be smart enough to finish my sentence. You must think of the last word of my sentence. And here's your clue: The word you think of must start with the first sound you hear in *baby* and *bear.* (repeat) Now I will read your sentence: At the store the baby bear bought a . (Count any word starting with b that fits the sentence.)

____ **50.** Here's your very last case, Madam (or Sir) Detective. To solve this case you must make up your own sentence about a sick sailor. Here are your clues: (Check on their understanding after each clue.)

a. Your sentence must have at least four words.

b. Your sentence must start with the same "little sound" as the first sound in *sick* and *sailor.*

c. Your sentence should begin this way: The sick sailor .

*The Phonological Awareness Interview in Box 4.1 has been copyrighted by Dr. Frank May and Dr. Sylvia Dean but may be copied for your own teaching convenience. It is against the law for anyone to use it for commercial benefit. It is available for sale to school districts and other agencies and may be purchased in quantities of ten or more through the publisher.

Myth 4, Part E: Positive Intervention Designed to Compensate for Teaching Phonics before Phonemic Awareness

Use the Phonological Awareness Interview for generating your own instructional lessons. For example, Box 4.2 shows a way of adapting part of the Phonological Awareness Interview.

BOX 4.2

Lessons on Phoneme Awareness: Recognizing Phonemes within Words

Lesson 1. Words with Three Phonemes

____ **1.** How many little sounds do you hear in the word *cat?*
What are those three sounds in *cat*? [/c/+/a/+/t/]

____ **2.** How many little sounds do you hear in the name *Jack*?
What are those three sounds in *Jack*? [sounds, not letters]

____ **3.** How many little sounds in *run*?
What are those three sounds in *run*? [sounds, not letters]

____ **4.** How many little sounds in the silly word **mup*?
What are those three sounds in **mup*?

____ **5.** Think of a real word that has three little sounds in it.

____ **6.** Make up a silly word that has three little sounds in it.

(Now have them make up more words with three little sounds.)

b. Words with Four Phonemes

____ **1.** How many little sounds do you hear in the word *scat?*
What are those four sounds in *scat*? [/s/+/k/+/a/+/t/]

____ **2.** How many little sounds do you hear in the word *crack?*
What are those four sounds in *crack*?

_____ **3.** How many little sounds in *plane*? [sounds not letters]

What are those four sounds in *plane*?

_____ **4.** How many little sounds in the silly word **trid*?

What are those four sounds in **trid*?

_____ **5.** Think of a real word that has four little sounds in it.

_____ **6.** Make up a silly word that has four little sounds in it.

(Now play a game with two teams. The teacher gives a word, and students take turns saying the exact four little sounds in the word.)

c. Words with Five Phonemes

_____ **1.** How many little sounds do you hear in the word *splat?*

What are those five sounds in *splat*?

_____ **2.** How many little sounds do you hear in the word *flaps*?

What are those five sounds in *flaps*?

_____ **3.** How many little sounds in *sprain*?

What are those five sounds in *sprain*?

_____ **4.** How many little sounds in the silly word **stimp*?

What are those five sounds in **stimp*?

_____ **5.** Think of a real word that has five little sounds in it.

_____ **6.** Make up a silly word that has five little sounds in it.

_____ **7.** How many BIG SOUNDS (syllables)do you hear in *ap-ple*? In *help-ful*?

_____ **8.** How many little sounds do you hear in *robin*?

_____ **9.** What are those five sounds?

____ **10.** Think of another two-syllable word with five little sounds.

____ **11.** Think of a two-syllable silly word with five sounds.

So, there you have it. An example of the many teaching ideas you can generate just by studying the Phoneme Awareness Interview, described in detail in this chapter.

For an excellent source of additional teaching ideas for phonological awareness, you may wish to order the inexpensive paperback by Lita Ericson and Moira Faser Juliebo called *The Phonological Awareness Handbook for Kindergarten and Primary Teachers*. It was published in 1998 by the International Reading Association, 800 Barksdale Road, P.O. Box 8139, Newark, DE, 19714–8139, USA, www.reading.org

CHAPTER

5 The Fifth Myth of Reading

Myth 5, Part A: Reading Comprehension Is Nothing More or Less than the Ability to Answer Questions about Text.

In this chapter you and I will examine the most important consequence of effective reading instruction: the wide-spectrum ability called "reading comprehension." This complex, mysterious capability is fundamental for effective communication in today's society.

Reading Comprehension: It's Not Indicated by Right Answers

Minicase 1. Alvino correctly answers all of your questions related to a passage he has just read aloud. Can you be sure that he has comprehended what the author said?

a. No. Answers to most questions from the teacher may be more related to an excellent memory than to the conceptual and motivational processes of comprehending what is read.
b. Furthermore, every time a teacher has to help the novice with a word, she provides more information for his memory bank, which can be used a few moments later for answering the questions she asks him.
c. This, in turn, fools adults like me into thinking that any student who can answer all those questions has surely demonstrated a high degree of reading comprehension. (Have you ever noticed that the word *adult* is very similar to *a dolt*? That's what I've felt myself to be at times.)
d. In addition, questions are often worded in ways that confuse the students. Therefore, we end up with a measure of how well they

couldn't comprehend our questions, but not necessarily how well they comprehended the author.

e. And what about those questions that are worded so foolishly they give the answer away? In this case, what are we really measuring? Comprehension of the author's message or the student's ability to listen for cues that come from the wording of the question? Whose set of cues is the reader receiving, the author's or the teacher's?

f. Comprehension occurs at the moment when your student is actually reading (or trying to). If you want to check on comprehension, and not just memory, you'll need to listen carefully to exactly where he understands and where he doesn't. You'll also need to observe the strategies he uses to create understanding or to deal with his lack of understanding.

What Can We Use instead of Questions, Then?

Assessing a student's actual reading comprehension ability needs to be done in ways that are more concrete and on the spot, and therefore more valid and instructive. For example:

1. Collaborative miscue analysis: The student and teacher problem-solve together as to why a word substitute doesn't fit the author's meaning, or why a particular word is difficult to decode.
2. Collaborative examination of his long-term literacy portfolio, including his coded miscue-analysis records and journal entries. What is his trend over time toward
    a. Correcting his own miscues?
    b. Not correcting false substitutes?
    c. Using strategies to decode difficult passages?
    d. Not using comprehension strategies flexibly?
    e. Creating mental images of what he is reading?
3. Teaching your student to think aloud as he reads. Tape record two or three sessions to study strategies he is using and not using.
4. Teacher observations of his ability to contribute his version of the author's meanings, stimulated by "What do you think the author means by that?" or "What does the character mean by that?"
5. Observations of the degree to which he can read "between the lines" to make his own inferences (and to express them to you).

6. Observations or tape recordings of his ability to retell the essence of a story or article he has just read (without being questioned).
7. Observations of his ability to read lines of a play and meaningfully act out the part he is assigned.

Why Not Use Standardized Tests Instead?

Minicase 2. Ramona gets a high comprehension score on a standardized reading test. Can you now be certain that her reading comprehension is above average?

Not really. Standardized group tests rely primarily on question-answering of the worst kind, guessing which one of the multiple choices the test administrator thinks is correct (among four alternatives that may be shallow, misleading, or even culturally biased).

> The typical standardized group test does not measure the ability to engage in purposeful reading for information or entertainment. It measures, as we all probably know, the ability to take multiple-choice tests.

And those are just two of many reasons for the lack of validity so easily observed in standardized group tests.

Smooth Reading and Intonation: A Better Indicator Than Questions?

Minicase 3. Edward reads out loud every word in a passage—quickly, smoothly, accurately, and with the proper intonation. Doesn't that mean he comprehends what he's reading?

The only thing it means, for sure, is that Edward knows how to play the school game of "Reading Out Loud." Although such game playing is an important survival skill, it does not provide a convincing sign that he actually comprehends the author's message. I have worked with many neophytes who have fooled me with fast, smooth, and well-intonated reading. I have observed many other students who have fooled their teachers by the use of their marvelous sight word memory and their ability to guess words on the basis of the title, picture, or teacher's introduction of the story or article.

Edward's overall performance would suggest to me that he has a good sight vocabulary and a sharp awareness of syntax, two talents that are certainly ingredients of the much richer stew called "reading comprehension." Yet, those two skills, even combined, are definitely not equivalent to reading comprehension.

Teachers' Grades on Reading: A Superior Indicator of "Reading Comprehension"?

Minicase 4: Margie's Father. "Margie received an A in reading on her last report card. This time Margie received an A+. As far as I'm concerned, that proves my little Margie is getting the very best reading instruction possible."

I'm happy for you, sir, but I'm afraid that reading comprehension has very little to do with our 'branding-iron' method of student evaluation. The research on grading students has shown me something you might have noticed during your own high school and college years: Reading grades are often based on the compatibility among student, parent, and teacher. And, I'm sorry to say, sometimes on their mutual ethnic or economic status.

Reading Comprehension: What *Is* It, Then?

First, a more specific question I've been asked many times. "I've heard that reading comprehension is a process and not a product. Is that right?"

The gist of my varied answers to that question goes something like this: Like every other *process* we engage in, reading is also a *product.* A painting is a product *produced* through a process and *viewed* through another process. A symphony is a product *produced* through a process and *listened to* through another process. For every process there is a product, even if it's nothing more than a good feeling (which usually interacts with the process in such a way that you carry on the process again and again). Likewise, each *reading* act is a set of interacting processes and products. (The same is true for every writing act.) It is probable that every second of reading *comprehension* includes an interacting process and product.

> This amazing interaction, as you may already know, is one that connects the ideas, images, and experiences of a writer with prior ideas, images, and experiences of a reader. For instance, the writer, Carolyn, thinks and writes: "My uncle brought me a present for my birthday." The reader, James, interacts with the writer by reading and thinking about his own images, ideas, and experiences related to *favorite, uncle, birthday,* and "someone who once gave him a present."

Pathways of Communication between Reader and Author

The decades of research on reading comprehension point to the probability that reading comprehension takes place when both writer and reader have done a good job of communicating. (In Chapter 6, you and I can talk about the writer's communication responsibilities and how teachers can compensate for writers like me who sometimes communicate very poorly. In this chapter, though, I'd like to concentrate on how a good reader communicates with a writer. As a reader you:

1. Communicate by staying attentive to five indispensable and interrelated cue systems:
   a. The schematic system of language (your stored minitheories about life in general and language in particular);
   b. The semantic system of language (author's word meanings);
   c. The syntactic system of language (author's word arrangements);
   d. The phonemic system of oral language (the smallest language sounds);
   e. The graphemic system of written language (letter patterns that correspond with and represent the phonemic system). Put system d and e together and voilà, you have the graphophonic system referred to as "phonics."

2. Communicate through parallel recognition of all five cues (see Chapter 2 on parallel wiring of the brain, "like Christmas lights").
3. Communicate by way of making inferences while "reading between the lines."
4. Communicate through experimentation with open-ended, flexible reading comprehension strategies. (Problem solving of any kind requires, by its very nature, open-ended, flexible thinking.)
5. Communicate by means of noticing authors' ways of constructing both fiction and nonfiction, through (a) their story structure, such as the character's nature, the conflicts or challenges set before this character, the appropriate setting for such challenges, and (b) their explanation structure—methods used for explaining, such as sequence, cause and effect, problem and solution. Noticing these structures allows the reader to *stay* with

the author rather than *stray* from the author. Noticing those structures also allows the reader to predict what's coming next.

Achieving Reading Comprehension by Attending to Multiple Cues

Carolyn's following sentence provides us with an example of how James has to apply his brain power through parallel recognition of multiple types of cues associated with her message: "My favorite uncle brought me a present for my birthday."

The Schema Cues. James must quickly scan his memory bank of "schemas"—minitheories, notions, stereotypes, and assumptions developed about the world during his lifetime so far. One schema stored in James's mind is this: "My favorite uncle is a cool guy." This broad schema, of course, is made up of minischemas associated with the concept of *my,* with *favorite, uncle, is, cool, guy,* and even with *a* guy rather than *the* guy."

As a skillful reader, James quickly recalls the *essence* of the experiences, schemas, concepts, and feelings that have been expressed by Carolyn in that single sentence. More specifically, he recalls the essence of prior memories about (1) "My favorite uncle," (2) "brought me a present," and (3) "for my birthday." Not only that, James recalls using or hearing the sound of the words, phrases, and sentence patterns that are now being used by Carolyn. As you can see, then, our schematic memories are based on both the actual experiences and the language patterns associated with those kinds of experiences.

The Semantic and Syntactic Cues. What triggers the schematic memory system we just discussed? Two major cues: the meaningful words (semantic cues), and the meaningful word arrangements (syntactic cues), which the writer (or speaker) offers to the reader (or listener). In short:

> In comes the writer's message with its particular word meanings, word choices, sentence arrangements, and experiential shadings. Out come the reader's interpretations and inferences based on prior knowledge, language mastery, and life experiences.

In this way, then, Carolyn's sentence is truly comprehended: "My favorite uncle" is comprehended; "brought me a present" is comprehended; "for my birthday" is comprehended. The entire "sentence," and its many interrelationships are comprehended.

The Phoneme and Grapheme Systems. But wait a minute! Such speedy and intricate comprehension didn't take place without the vital help of two other cues: the graphemes Carolyn used for coding that sentence, and the phonemes James used for *decoding* that sentence. (Please refer to Chapters 3 and 4 for any necessary review of those two vital cues we communicators provide for each other.)

Inferential Thinking: The Life Blood of Reading Comprehension

For most of my career I have encountered an almost universal mental block among teachers (including myself), a block that I have dubbed "inferphobia." It's not that we teachers are averse to making hasty inferences or assumptions, or drawing quick conclusions, or even making swift judgments. We probably do those kinds of things far more than the general population. (We have to in order to survive.)

It's just that when we're asked to "teach students how to make inferences as they read," our minds customarily freeze from fright. We grudgingly plod to the teacher's manual and search for questions labeled "inferential." The stingy manual provides us only one inferential question for the story our students are about to read. It goes like this: "Where was Wild Willie?"

Well, that doesn't sound like making an inference. It sounds like nothing more than remembering what the author said. So we go to the story to find out where Wild Willie was. The author doesn't say! She just says,

> The sun was going down. The air was hot and Wild Willie was afraid. Never had he been in such a dry, hot place.

We sigh with relief. We have found a bona fide inferential-thinking question to ask our students. We smile, knowing that our students will have to infer that Willie is in a desert, because the author refuses to say the word *desert.* "Whew!" we say. "Thank goodness we have a teacher's manual."

Teaching Reading Comprehension through Inferential Thinking

Instead of thumbing through your teacher's manual every time you want to encourage inferential thinking, let me remind you of just how simple it is to get students to *comprehend* better through inferential thinking. We'll take the story of "The Three Bears," one that's known by nearly every culture on Earth.

To teach novices how to infer, you simply make them conscious of what we humans do all the time: When someone *speaks* to us, we listen not only to the literal message but to *the messages between the lines.* In like manner, when we read, we "listen" within our heads to the *author* and infer the messages left between the lines. When authors write stories (or parents tell stories), they don't tell you everything. To keep from boring you out of your mind with too many details, *they subconsciously leave empty slots for your imagination to fill in.* For example, here's the second and third sentences of "The Three Bears."

2. One morning the mommy bear put some hot cereal into three bowls—a great big bowl, a middle sized bowl, and a wee little bowl.
3. The cereal was too hot to eat, so the three bears went for a walk in the forest.

How in the world are you going to have your students do any inferential thinking with that?! It's easy. *Just look for the empty slots.* What did the author leave to your imagination?

Slot #1: Did he tell you where the mommy bear was? ("Nonsense.")

Slot #2: Did he tell you where she placed the bowls? ("Never.")

Slot #3: Or which bowl belonged to each bear? ("Of course not.")

(The quotes above are from Colonel Pickering in *My Fair Lady.*)

With all three slots, the "author" of "The Three Bears" relied on you to fill in with your own imagination, which is largely based on your own prior experiences and your own invented schemas about the way the world works.

So, we now have three empty slots, and your students have to semiconsciously fill them with three inferences. As you read this story with them you simply ask them natural conversational questions like these: What part of the house was the mommy bear in, do you think? Where in the kitchen do you suppose she placed the bowls? Who do you think had the middle sized bowl?

> Questions like those (asked in a conversational, rather than testing manner) require a student to infer details or ideas that the author left out. Inferential questions like those also get students to picture in their mind what the author is talking about. Consistent use of inference-based conversational questions can help students get in the habit of reading between the lines of text, in the same way those same students intuitively listen between the lines of speech. This form of inferential thinking, in turn, can strengthen their overall reading comprehension ability.

The Use of Subskills as Decoding and Comprehension Strategies

For two or three decades, reading comprehension was treated as if it were a grab bag of tricks, called either "skills" or "subskills." Each subskill was supposed to be learned and mastered separately. Why? Because it was believed that "logically" the addition of all the subskills automatically and arithmetically added up to a sum, the overall skill called (drum roll please):

r—e—a—d—i—n—g

c—o—m—p—r—e—h—e—n—s—i—o—n.

In many schools every child had a card that was punched after each subskill was "mastered" (with mastery based on short little unreliable test scores). The subskills for "decoding words" filled several punch cards, while the subskills for "reading comprehension" might fill only one or two. The comprehension subskills included so-called separate capabilities. The student:

1. Can follow and remember a sequence with (a) directions, (b) events in a story, (c) serial information such as the "water cycle";
2. Can find and remember important details about where and when;

3. Can find and remember important details about who and why;
4. Can find and remember important details about what and how;
5. Can determine and remember the author's main idea in a paragraph or section;
6. Can determine and remember the cause and effect in (a) a story or (b) a description of an event;
7. Can distinguish between fantasy and fact presented by an author.

Teachers, administrators, professors, and other educators learned to perceive those noble and reasonable goals as if they were almost physical skills like knitting or pounding in a nail. (I assure you that I'm not making fun of other educators. After all, I was a believer in that "logical" approach for a few years myself.)

The Use of Strategies to Achieve Reading Comprehension

Slowly we have come out of our tightly woven cocoon made of tightly separated subskills and have begun to fly. To fly well, though, requires a very different perspective on reading. Our former perception of reading was similar to the process of gathering little round stones, cramming them into a pretty glass jar, and displaying them on the coffee table. Our present perception is more like flying into puzzling clouds of bumpy long words and large unfamiliar ideas, then creating problem-solving strategies to either go through or around them. In brief we have substituted subskills for comprehension strategies. This in turn has caused us to perceive reading as an open-ended, multifaceted, flexible, problem-solving experience.

But just what do we mean by comprehension strategies? First of all, we mean problem-solving acts such as these: (1) predicting the next words, (2) confirming our prediction, (3) changing our prediction if necessary, (4) correcting our own miscues, (5) using substitutions that get us closer to the author's meaning, (6) using omissions and insertions to make the author's language sound more like our own language, and (7) stalling for think-time by repeating words and phrases.

Reading comprehension is achieved partially through those seven comprehension strategies. But by "reading comprehension," we also mean other, deeper, strategies that can enhance our understanding. The high-flying "active comprehender" is predicting not only the next words but the next idea, the next step—or with fiction, the next conflict the hero is going to face. By the time the active comprehender of a mystery has finished the third chapter, she's predicting the ending of the story! She is already heavily into the process of confirming her hunches about who the murderer actually was. She is arguing with a suspect's point of view and searching for flaws in his alibi. She is doing all of this within seconds rather than minutes. In sum, she's most likely using her mind the way it was meant to be used—creatively, with room for doubt, with concern and advice for either the main character or the author, and particularly with her own purposes clearly out there in the front line.

Are Comprehension Strategies Easy to Teach?

Judging from the enthusiasm of educators in the 1980s and 1990s for specific reading comprehension strategies, one would think that the research would say, "Absolutely!" to that question. As you'll see in Part B, experimental research on the effectiveness of specific and prescribed strategies is encouraging but not as conclusive as the publishers of basal readers and other anthologies would like us to believe. Unfortunately, they've caught on to the word "strategy," but not always to the nature of "strategy."

A reading comprehension strategy is not often a recipe or step-by-step construction plan (like those you never can follow when you receive one of those infamous "kits" you have to unbox and put together). A comprehension strategy refers more to a thinking process than a set of rules. As another caution, let me suggest that any strategy or procedure, to be effective, needs to be fueled by the student's personal drive to satisfy certain goals and needs. For example, "I'm dying to read this book my boy friend gave to me. He thinks I'm just like the main character," or "I know I can find the answer to my problem in here," or "Maybe this will help me become a computer expert some day."

> Whether a strategy is military or educational, it is an art of spontaneously creating and implementing plans for reaching a goal. In the case of a reading strategy, the goal is that of communicating so well with an author that you satisfy your academic and personal needs.

Overcoming Blocks to Teaching Flexible Comprehension Strategies

What may be blocking teachers the most is the cultural expectation that we all should have the same teaching goals and use the same methods for all students. The feeling I often get from Curriculum Guides, Teaching Guides, or from professors' syllabi is that we should teach all of our students the same comprehension strategies, teach them precise steps like those of putting a kit together, or even like formulas of mathematicians, physicists, and chemists.

Besides cultural expectations blocking our way to flexibility, we may simply not be comfortable standing up in front of others and modeling how we personally use strategies when we read. Most of us are not used to that. If we have to teach comprehension strategies at all, we'd prefer to do it in recipe fashion: "Grease the pan, set the oven for 350, mix all dry ingredients, add wet ingredients, and stir with a very expensive French whisk."

This form of precision and inflexibility is in sharp contrast with teachers I've observed who have let go of their reticence and "act/think" right out loud in front of their students. The goal, in their modeling, is to inspire their protégés: to create, share, and experiment with their own home-made or borrowed comprehension strategies. These teachers display their own flexible methods without making them out as prescriptions for curing cancer of the mind. Here are some examples of their think-aloud, modeled strategies, often carried on spontaneously during a reading lesson:

1. How they motivate themselves to read something (and what happens to their comprehension when they forget to stay motivated). *"Why do I want to read this?"* or *"Why do I need to read this?"*

2. How they prepare their minds for searching in the text for ideas or stories that accomplish or satisfy their goal or need. *"What am I looking for?"*

3. How they challenge themselves to predict the ending, the next disaster, the next argument of the author, always with the goal of receiving pleasure from predicting accurately. *"What's going to happen next?"* or *"What idea is coming up?"* or *"What's the point she's trying to make?"*

4. How they make up for their temporary loss of attention to their reasons for reading a selection. *"Am I reading this or just passing my eyes over it?"*

5. How they often change their goals midstream, as they read. *"I think I've got all I can get from this author. This makes me want to find an-*

other book on this topic," or *"I need to slow down if I'm going to understand this."*

6. How they openly sympathize or disagree with the author or characters or ideas. *"Yes, Cherie, go for it!"* or *"No, Jim, don't do it!"* or *"That idea doesn't make sense, George."*

7. How they recall and relate their own experiences to those of the author or the characters. *"Wow, I've done that myself."* or *"I think he must mean like those red things I bought at Nordstrom's."*

None of the above modeling sessions are designed to present a precise recipe, but instead to show what problem solving looks like. For more generalized strategies refer to those described in the Research Review by Dole, Duffy, Rochler, and Pearson in Part B. (For more examples of specific comprehension strategies, see the list in Part E.)

Concluding Remarks

Reading comprehension is both a process and a product of communicating with another person, a person who has bothered to put what she or he has to say or tell in written form. The writer and reader, each at a different time and place, of course, must want to stop whatever else they are thinking about and communicate. The product side of "reading comprehension" requires a variety of highly flexible processes called "comprehension strategies." All strategies aim toward the solving of academic or personal needs and the gaining of self-power and self-confidence.

Myth 5, Part B: Research That Refutes the Fifth Myth of Reading

Once again, I could have used the simplistic method of selecting competently developed research studies by choosing references only from the last ten years. Please note the fallacy of such selection. The period between 1974 and 1991 (and particularly during the 1980s) provided teachers and other educators with at least 90% of the studies on Reading Strategies. Very few studies of merit have been published since 1991. Why is this so? Partly because researchers and financial supporters of research have accomplished so much that they've gone on to more prevalent problems to solve. It's also because published results of studies on teaching a particular strategy or concept tend to float into shore on a large popularity wave. This wave displays its power for several years, then turns mainly into tiny driblets of unresearched and mildly researched afterthought.

A Review of Research on the Validity of Questions

McKenna, M. C. (1983). Informal reading inventories: A review of the issues. *Reading Teacher, 36*, 670–679.

Conclusions

1. Studies on comprehension questions indicate that they are often not reliable indicators of how well a student has understood a selection of text.
2. One set of questions on a selection will place a student at the instructional level; another set of questions on the same selection will place her at the frustration or independent level.
3. Questions are less likely to measure comprehension of text than they are to measure memory—of what she has read, of what the teacher pronounced for her, of answers to similar questions, or of background experiences.

Comments. I would like to add two final cautions about using correctly answered questions as a measure of reading comprehension: (1) Because of the different schemas that people carry around with them, there is no foreseeable way for us very human educators to come up with questions that measure the difficulty of a passage for every student who reads out loud during a single session with a single informal reading inventory. (2) Counting the number of "correctly" answered questions (whether the questions are teacher-made or created for a standardized test) is an invalid procedure (not true-to-life, not true to the nature of reading) for determining a student's reading comprehension ability.

An Integration of the Research Findings on Reading Comprehension, Use of Comprehension Strategies, and Methods of Teaching

Dole, J. A., Duffy, G. G., Roehler, L. R., and Pearson, P. D. (1991). Moving from the old to the new: Research on reading comprehension instruction. *Review of Educational Research, 61*, 2, 239–264.

Conclusions

1. Reading comprehension is not a set of separate skills that we can master. It is a much more complex interaction between the reader's knowledge, her strategies, and the author's ability to communicate.
2. Reading comprehension is based primarily on two characteristics of readers: (a) their prior knowledge [schema development], and (b) how effectively [and flexibly] they use comprehension strategies to get at the author's messages.
3. Five general comprehension strategies have emerged from research on the cognitive (problem solving) aspects of reading. All of these strategies have been successfully taught to learners:

   Strategy #1: Determining Importance. Purposefully searching for main ideas, themes, desired information, author biases, major relationships among author's ideas, the story structures, and explanation structures used by the author.

   Strategy #2: Summarizing Information. Going beyond the search for importance to creating the reader's own synthesis about facts, ideas, or stories, a slowly learned task for most students, consisting of selecting, deleting, condensing, and integrating information into a message similar to the author's message but more personal and meaningful to the reader.

   Strategy #3: Drawing Inferences. Actively engaging in the crucial process of reading between the lines and constructing information based on the reader's prior experience and knowledge.

   Strategy #4: Generating Questions. Asking questions of oneself or peers that help the reader determine or confirm information such as the story structure, the forms of explanation, or the main ideas.

   Strategy #5: Monitoring Comprehension. Regulating and revising comprehension strategies during the process of reading; noticing and correcting reading problems and other inconsistencies as they occur.

4. Explaining the usefulness and relevance of what is being taught can help motivate students to read for the purpose of comprehending the author's ideas, and therefore to use effective comprehension strategies during that process.

Comments

This was a highly comprehensive review on the most effective and teachable comprehension strategies. However, you should be aware that the populations chosen for the reviewed studies included primary, middle school, and high school students. Let's move on to another review with populations of young elementary school students only to see if there are any differences between one age level and another.

A Review of Successful Strategies for Elementary School Students

Pressley, M., Johnson, C. J., Symons, S., McGoldrick, J. A., & Kurita, J. A. (1989). Strategies that improve children's memory and comprehension of text. *Elementary School Journal, 90,* 1, 3–32.

Conclusions

1. These reading comprehension strategies have been demonstrated by research to be suitable for learning even by elementary school students:
   - **a.** Summarizing (e.g., paragraphs with only one sentence);
   - **b.** Constructing vivid images of what they are reading;
   - **c.** Using mnemonic devices to remember unfamiliar concepts;
   - **d.** Using story grammar to predict main character, setting, next conflict, and resolution;
   - **e.** Generating questions for peers and that require inferential thinking;
   - **f.** Answering self questions or peer questions by looking back at prior text for proof;
   - **g.** Using prior knowledge as a means of constructing their own examples of author's concepts and generalizations.

2. Teaching these strategies requires certain instructional procedures:
   - **a.** Teach one strategy thoroughly before going on to another;
   - **b.** Teach how to modify strategies when one doesn't work;
   - **c.** Emphasize the usefulness and relevance of each strategy;
   - **d.** Teach directly, explicitly, and extensively;
   - **e.** Allow for practice in the context of regular lessons in reading, social studies, science, and other curricula.

Comments. You might have noticed how familiar these strategies began to sound to you after reading about the previous studies in Part B and the ideas in Part A.

Research Support for Strategic Reading Comprehension from the View of the "Information Processing Framework"

Pressley, M., Goodchild, F., Fleet, J., Zajchowski, R., & Evans, E. D. (1989). The challenges of classroom strategy instruction. *Elementary School Journal, 89,* 3, 301–342.

Conclusions

1. Psychologists who use the "information processing framework" are probably correct in the following assumptions:
   a. Information is filtered, retained, and remembered in our sensory organs before it is transported into our short-term memory.
   b. The information in our short-term memory disappears unless it is "processed" through rehearsing or through other motivated use of the information.
   c. Some of the short-term information passes into long-term storage of our prior knowledge, schemas, images, theories, biases, and strategies.
   d. These strategies are a major form of "software" that allow us to intentionally, purposefully carry on our various problem-solving endeavors. For instance, young children often use the strategy of counting on their fingers to reach the sum of two numbers. As another example, good readers use a strategy such as returning to the previous paragraph to understand what the author is getting at or what the main character just did. A further example would be the music student who learns to use a mnemonic device of F-A-C-E (face) to remember notes in the treble clef.
2. Students need to be shown, not lectured on how strategies can help them meet their academic requirements and personal goals.
3. Teacher education needs (pruning and thinning) to make room for specific and intensive training in how to develop young students' ability to use comprehension strategies.

Using the Cloze Technique to Teach the Strategy of Integrating Prior Knowledge with Text Information

Dewitz, P., Carr, E. M., & Patberg, J. (1987). Effects of inference training on comprehension and comprehension monitoring. *Reading Research Quarterly 22,* 1, 99–119.

Results and Conclusions

1. Teachers can successfully use deletions in a "cloze" test as a means of showing learners strategies for integrating prior knowledge with text information.
2. The inferential comprehension scores of the experimental group (using the procedure above) were significantly superior to those of the control group.
3. The experimental group also had significantly superior scores on a test that estimated their metacognitive awareness (of how well they were understanding the author).

The Kamehameha Early Education Project (KEEP): Direct Instruction of Comprehension Strategies

Au, K. H. & Mason, J. M. (1981). Social organizational factors in learning to read. The balance of rights hypotheses. *Reading Research Quarterly, 17,* 1, 115–152.

Results and Conclusions

1. Several ingredients are required for a reading program that uses direct teaching methods for explaining comprehension strategies to high-risk children:
   a. Daily direct teaching of comprehension strategies;
   b. Specific and positive praise for students' efforts to learn a strategy;
   c. Continual monitoring and guiding of their practice;
   d. Opportunities to communicate in small groups in ways consistent with their culture;
   e. Interaction between teacher and students that is relaxed and supportive;
   f. Teachers creating discussion questions that tap a variety of comprehension levels and thinking processes, encourage speculation, and require the use of prior knowledge and specific experiences.

g. Teachers actively seeking their students' improvement in answering questions on comprehension tests.
2. By experiencing those seven instructional ingredients, the high-risk children were able to perform significantly better on comprehension tests than comparison students in phonics programs with an emphasis on phonics.

• *Comments.* Their relaxed and flexible procedures, balanced with direct teaching in a caring mode, make a great deal of sense. Yet, their approach to assessing the effectiveness of their procedures makes less sense from the research standpoint. With the experimental teachers actively seeking their students' improvement in answering questions on comprehension tests, it is to be expected that the experimental group would do better than the control group on standardized comprehension tests.

Direct and Highly Explicit Teaching of Comprehension Strategies

Duffy, G., Roehler, L., Meloth, M., Vavrus, L., Book, C., Putnam, J., & Wesselman, R. (1986). *Reading Research Quarterly, 21,* 3, 237–252.

Conclusions

1. Poor readers increased their awareness of the teacher's instructional goals.
2. Poor readers became capable of outperforming control students on the Michigan Educational Assessment Program (MEAP), an assessment more in line with the actual instruction than the standardized comprehension test.
3. Poor readers can learn how to use comprehension strategies on their own.

Comments on the Previous Studies and Reviews

I hope you're as pleased as I am that many educators have been carefully studying the nature of strategies and of strategy instruction. These researchers, however, have been almost forced by present cultural expectations and by tradition to rely on standardized test scores for their "results." This is in spite of the well-known lack of validity of such tests, particularly when they're used to assess problem solving and products and processes like reading.

Valid tests of reading ability assess more immediate, concrete, and personal progress, such as, "In the past month how much has Johnny improved in his abilities to (a) correct his own miscues, (b) predict what the author is going to say next, and (c) use his own prior knowledge to help him understand an author?

Actual reading and reading comprehension have very little to do with the oversimplified, overefficient act of choosing one of four possible "answers." Much better, much more valid studies can be developed that also use alternative assessments, such as the Michigan Educational Assessment Program (MEAP), an assessment more in line with the actual instruction than the standardized comprehension test, and, even more so, those on-the-spot procedures discussed in Part A of this chapter.

Myth 5, Part C: A Case Study Showing the Errors in Teacher Judgment Possible as a Result of the Fifth Myth

A Case Study of Tommy, the Story Maker

Tommy's middle name should have been Ernest. In every selection he read to me, he would use every muscle, breath, and strategy to create a story, not necessarily the author's story, but a story nevertheless.

Tommy, who was then seven-and-a-half, read five selections into my tape recorder. After reading each short selection, he answered six questions. I was amazed by what I thought was his superb reading comprehension ability—in spite of his fitful starts and stops, his heavy breathing, his frequent substitutions of his own word for the author's word, and his inability to decipher several words.

On the first three selections Tommy scored at the "independent comprehension level," answering every question correctly. On the last two selections he scored at the "instructional comprehension level," missing only one question on each. Percentagewise, his "comprehension scores" were: 100% for the preprimer book; 100% for the primer book; 100% for the Grade 1 book; 85.7% for the Grade 2 (first semester) book; and 83.3% for the Grade 2 (second semester) book.

On the one hand I was happy about his supposed "reading comprehension ability." You see, I had learned, through watching other teachers assess their students, that "reading comprehension" was nothing more or less than the ability to answer questions on text. So naturally I suggested to his teacher that Tommy be placed for reading instruction at the second grade (second half) reading level. That night, however, I felt a strong cerebral itch that kept me awake for what seemed like several hours. I kept asking myself, in a variety of ways, "If he was so good on comprehension, why did he struggle so much to get through the story?"

The next day, that same cerebral itch took me all the way to the city's university library. And that's when I first read Kenneth and Yetta Goodman's work on three related subjects: (1) miscue analysis, (2) a more valid definition of *comprehension*, and (3) some of the comprehension strategies that good and poor readers use.

Tommy taught me a great deal, and I'd like to invite you to learn from him as well. To avoid fatigue we'll study only one of the five selections he read to me. In the left column below is the author's message (or story). In the right column is Tommy's rendition of that message. Do notice how he sometimes created his own story rather than the author's. To me, this was a sign of progress at his age, for it showed me he was already predicting and problem solving as he read rather than merely reading word by word.

Author	**Tommy**
One hot day, Roy went on a boat ride.	One hot day, Roy went on a boat ride.
He went with his teacher and his school friends.	**and** he went with his teacher and his school friends.
It was cool on the water. And it was fun.	It was cool on the water. And it was fun.
The boat went by big city houses.	The boat went by big city houses.
Slow boats and fast boats	**Shop** boats—slow boats and fast boats
went by in the water.	went by in the water.
Roy saw a little boat pull a big boat.	Roy **was** a little boat **pulled by** a big boat.
Then it was time for lunch.	Then—**then** it was time for lunch.
Some children had lunch with them.	**Soon**—some children had lunch with them.
Some children had money for hot dogs.	Some children had money for hot dogs.

(continued)

Author	Tommy
All the children had milk. Roy had a hot dog.	All the children had milk. Roy had a hot dog.
His friend Max said,	His friend **Mac** said,
Look at the houseboat, Roy."	"Look at the houseboat, Roy."
Roy turned around fast.	Roy turned around fast.
His hot dog fell in the water.	His—**his** hot dog fell in the water.
"It fell!" said Roy. "My hot dog fell."	"It fell!" said Roy. "My hot dog fell."
"Now I have no hot dog. And I have no money."	"Now I have no hot dog. And I have no money."
"Here, Roy," said Max.	"**There**—here, Roy," said Mac.
He gave some money to Roy.	"**I have** some money," **said** Roy—to Roy.

What Can We Learn about Comprehension from Tommy? Subcase A

Tommy was almost errorless until he got to "Slow boats and fast boats went by in the water." Instead of "Slow boats" Tommy predicted "Shop boats" and then changed it to the author's "Slow boats." What do you suppose was going on in his mind?

Remember that the sentence before this one gave him vital information: "The boat went by big city houses." Do you see why he might have predicted "Shop boats" instead of "Slow boats." He subconsciously created his own story at this point (which showed me he had developed a sense of "story structure").

What I haven't told you yet is that Tommy lived in a big city. This fact made me suspect he was at the beginning stage, at least, of "using his prior knowledge and experience" as a major "comprehension strategy" for communicating with the author. But why did he bother to correct his substitution of *shop* for *slow*? Not because *shop* didn't make sense. It made perfect sense to this city boy who had seen so many shops. Then why did he correct it? Or, to put it a better way, "What strategies was he using that caused him to correct it?"

Actually, we can see that Tommy used four basic strategies at approximately the same time: semantic, schematic, graphophonic, and syntactic:

First Strategy. Predicting on the basis of semantic cues (word meanings) appearing in the previous sentence, i.e., "city houses."

A Second Simultaneous Strategy. Predicting on the basis of his prior knowledge, experience, and schema cues (minitheories regarding city life and boats).

A Third Simultaneous Strategy. Checking and changing his prediction because of the graphophonic cues: s-h-o-p versus s-l-o-w, and the differences in their sounds: /sh/ versus /s-l/ and /o-p/ versus /o/.

A Fourth Simultaneous Strategy. Making sure he followed the same syntax as the author. For example, he didn't change the order of the words in the sentence, nor did he change the relationship between adjective and noun (*shop boats—slow boats*). In addition, he didn't exchange the past tense, "Slow boats and fast boats went..." for the present tense, "Slow boats and fast boats go...." In short, it looks like Tommy might have an intuitive grasp of grammatical "rules" relating to syntax.

What Can We Learn about Comprehension from Tommy? Subcase B

So far, so good. Tommy is using the four most basic comprehension strategies successfully. In the next sentence we can watch him use all but one of those four. See if you can detect which one he ignores.

THE AUTHOR SAYS: Roy saw a little boat pull a big boat.

TOMMY SAYS: Roy was a little boat pulled by a big boat.

First Strategy. Predicting semantically? Yes, on all words but *was* for *saw*. His very reasonable prediction of *was* presented him with an exacting challenge, as far as communicating with the author.

Second Strategy. Predicting through prior knowledge and experience? Yes, he may have done this even with "Roy was a boat" because, after all, people do name their boats.

Third Strategy. Changing prediction because of graphophonic cues? No. He relied only on the semantic and syntactic cues and ignored the graphophonic cues of *saw* /saw/ versus *was* /wuz/. (On no other selection or words did he reverse the order of the letters in a word, so I felt certain that it was not a symptom of neurological dyslexia.)

Fourth Strategy. Following the same syntax as the author. What he did, instead, was to skillfully follow the syntax of his own story. Because Tommy changed "Roy saw" to "Roy was" he now had to follow his fourth strategy (syntax) by changing "Roy saw a little boat **pull** a big boat" to "Roy was a little boat **pulled by** a big boat." Does this show his comprehension of the writer's text? Decidedly not. But it does tell us that he's quite conscious of the crucial syntax strategy. Once he committed himself to "Roy **was** a little boat," he tossed graphophonic cues into the wind and made a nice little grammatical switch from *pull* to *pulled by.*

The Effect of All This on His "Comprehension"

Does this mean that Tommy got the answer wrong when he was asked a question about the boats? And consequently, did the question and answer technique cleverly uncover his lack of comprehension? No, he could have obtained the correct answer merely by paying attention to the wording of the question about boats.

For this topic he was asked a very leading question: "What did a little boat do?" Based on this wording, he could have easily thought something like this: "Oh, I guess it was the little boat doing the pulling and not the big boat." His actual answer was,"He pulled a big boat," thus blending his own story with the author's. Another possibility, of course, is that he glanced back at that strange sentence right after he had read it and realized he had the boats reversed in their positions.

At any rate, Tommy, along with many other children and adults, has taught me to be very suspicious of question-and-answer assessment of actual, on-the-spot reading comprehension. You might want to remember this from Part A:

Comprehension occurs at the time when your student is actually reading (or trying to). If you want to check his comprehension, and not just memory, you'll need to listen and observe carefully as to where in the passage he does understand and where he doesn't. You'll also need to observe the strategies he uses to create understanding or to deal with his lack of understanding.

What Can We Learn about Literature Comprehension from Tommy? Subcase C

Tommy's last lesson (that I'm going to show you) might be his most profound lesson for us. The author says, "He gave some money to Roy." Watch how Tommy again tells his own story: "I have some money," said Roy....

What do you think Tommy was thinking? (Here's some thinking time for you:.) No peeking ahead...

Okay, we're back together and I'm tempted to agree with you. The author visualized Max giving money to Roy. But Tommy visualized (and therefore predicted) that Roy was in the act of getting some money out of his pocket to give to Max (alias Mac). This error in visualization caused him to produce a line from, let's say, "Act 3, Scene 3," in which the main character of his play heroically but modestly says, "I have some money!" (Sort of like the hero in a melodrama, who bellows, "I'll pay the rent!")

Sticking with literary and economic matters for a moment longer, let's review the additional strategies Tommy used for comprehending a story.He used four of them: (1) identifying with the two main characters, (2) visualizing the action of the characters, (3) sensing the characters' precise needs or feelings, and (4) checking the text to see if he was correct in his predictions about the characters (but in Tommy's case, only enough to help him create a sensible story).

The question he was asked about the boats was, "Why did Max give Roy some money?" You see, of course, why he scored 100% on "comprehension" for this selection. The wording of the question made it a cinch.

The same four strategies Tommy used for a story can be modified for informational text: (1) *identifying* with (but not necessarily agreeing with) the author's descriptions or opinions, (2) *visualizing* the descriptions or steps or causes and effects, (3) *sensing* the biases and feelings of the author, and (4) *checking* on one's predictions that led to identifying, visualizing, and sensing (indentifying—visualizing—sensing—checking).

Tommy's Reading Comprehension: Nine Assessment Points

Probably the best procedure for assessing a student's reading comprehension is a frequent one-on-one collaboration between student and teacher, both of whom are looking for why the author's message is not understood at the moment. More specifically, they are collaboratively troubleshooting for the misunderstanding, using nine criteria. Is it:

1. Because of an irregular word like *knight* or a multisyllable word that is difficult to translate from letter patterns to sound patterns?
2. Because the words require greater spelling pattern decoding skill than the student now possesses? For example, has he mastered enough regular phonograms (rimes) or vowel patterns, as in **it** and *hit* (VC), **ant** and *pant* (VCC), **ace** and *face* (VCE), **eat** and *cheat* (VCC), or **he** and *she* (CV)?
3. Because the substitution just used by the student did not fit the grammar or the meaning of the author? (Author: Whish! The door opened all by itself!)—(Student: Which the door opened all by itself.)
4. Because the student can not sight-read at least the 100 most frequent words in the English language?
5. Because the student obviously needs phonemic awareness training before he goes any further?
6. Because his prior knowledge, experiences, and schema bank (minitheories about the world) need enriching before he can possibly communicate with the author (through discussion, visuals, objects)?
7. Because he has insufficiently mastered at least the four basic comprehension strategies: semantic, syntactic, graphophonic, schematic?
8. Because the student has no clear purpose or desire to read the chosen text?
9. Because he has not learned to attend to the crucial punctuation cues?

Those nine questions have been invaluable in my one-on-one work with neophyte readers, whether as a classroom teacher or as a reading specialist. Tommy had two stumbling blocks: number 2 above, spelling pattern decoding (graphophonics), and number 4 above, mastery of the most frequent sight words. Somehow he had pulled himself up by the bootstraps and learned how to strategize better than he had learned how to encode and decode. (Now there's an interesting study for someone: How did he do it? My suspicion is that Tommy's natural disposition had caused him to dash up the mountain without worrying about supplies.)

Maybe we've all had that disposition at times.

Myth 4, Part D: Assessment Tools for Detecting and Overcoming the Fifth Myth of Reading

Teacher's Self-Check List: Assessing Reading Comprehension Ability

This information is for your own self-evaluation and can be as confidential as you wish it to be. Use as much self-awareness as you can to determine what you actually do, rather than "should" or "want" to do.

______ **1.** I tend to determine students' comprehension of information text by asking questions that require memory of the author's main details and ideas.

______ **2.** I tend to determine students' comprehension of story text by asking questions that require memory of plot, main character, and setting.

______ **3.** I usually determine students' comprehension by checking their memory of main ideas and details at the end of the story or the information article.

______ **4.** I frequently collaborate with students in assessing each sentence or paragraph to help them evaluate their own comprehension or lack of comprehension.

______ **5.** I ask my students more for their inferences or interpretations than I do for their memory of the author's text.

______ **6.** I like to have students specifically analyze, out loud, why they might be having trouble reading and what they might do about it.

______ **7.** I calmly stop my students shortly after they create a false substitute for the author's word, and ask them if their word fits what the author is saying. If it doesn't, I have them check the author's meaning and the letter patterns.

______ **8.** I praise students even more for demonstrating their comprehension than for reading each word correctly.

______ **9.** I usually model any comprehension strategy that I introduce to them.

______ **10.** I have them feel very comfortable with a strategy before moving on to a new strategy.

______ **11.** I teach some strategies more thoroughly than others because they are far more important for students to learn and use.

______ **12.** I do my best assessing of comprehension by asking students to explain why they think they made a false substitute or a no-show.

______ **13.** I notice when a question I ask may assess memory much more certainly than comprehension.

______ **14.** I use a variety of on-task comprehension assessments because I don't trust questions and answers to give me the whole picture.

______ **15.** I sometimes forget that some students do well on questions because of the cues they pick up from the question asked or from their own background.

______ **16.** I sometimes ask a student who skillfully self-corrects to model for the other students. This student explains why she miscued and how she corrected the miscue, i.e., what strategies she used.

______ **17.** I try to build each student's comprehension ability through the selection of interesting, relevant, and only moderately challenging text.

______ **18.** My chief goal is to help students admire authors as writers and themselves as readers.

Collaborative Check List for Use with Portfolio

(Notice that decoding is a crucial strategy for reading comprehension.)

______ **1.** Recognizes high-frequency irregular words e.g., *knight* or *done*.

______ **2.** Separates multisyllable words into recognizable phonograms, syllables, or endings.

______ **3.** Recognizes on sight most of the high-frequency phonograms (rimes).

______ **4.** Can decode (through onset insertion) most of the "family words" that have the same phonogram (with the same spelling).

______ **5.** Recognizes on sight at least four of the five regular vowel patterns: VC (*it, pit, spit, split*); VCC (*ink, sink, blink, shrink*); VCE (*ice, rice, spice, splice*); VVC (*ail, mail, frail, quail*); CV (*my, fly, cry, spy, spry*), (*be, me, he, she, we*), (*no, go, pro, co-, ho*).

______ **6.** Usually notices when his substitution does not fit the grammar or the meaning of the author, then independently makes a self-correction.

______ **7.** Can sight-read all of the 100 most frequent words in the English language.

______ **8.** Demonstrates awareness of phonemes and how to mentally blend or segment them in order to spell and read.

______ **9.** Actively participates with teacher and peers in enriching his prior knowledge, experiences, and schema bank (minitheories about the world) before he begins a new reading experience.

______ **10.** Demonstrates the most basic set of comprehension strategies of simultaneously using the four cues: semantic, syntactic, graphophonic, schematic.

______ **11.** Demonstrates his awareness of flexible strategies such as the cloze technique called "fill in the blank." (Described earlier in Part B and later in Part E.)

______ **12.** Collaborates with the teacher in developing a clear purpose and desire to read the chosen story, poem, song, or information.

______ **13.** Has mastered the crucial punctuation signals for both reading and writing: capital letter, period, comma, question mark, exclamation mark.

A Quick Estimate of Comprehension and Text Difficulty

Whenever you need an efficient, practical way to estimate a student's actual comprehension of the text she is reading, remember to pay attention to only two types of miscues: (1) her substitutions that do not fit the author's meaning, and (2) her inability to independently decode a word within 5 to 7 seconds.

If she consistently engages in those two specific miscues more than 5% of the time (more than 1 out of every 20 words), you can be reasonably certain her present reading comprehension has reached her frustration level. Probably she needs to read selections that are easier, more in tune with her experiential background, and especially more complimentary to her self-confidence as a learner and her self-image as a reader.

Myth 5, Part E: Positive Intervention for Helping Teachers and Students Move Past the Fifth Myth

Intervention Ideas

I. Teach students to use the four basic strategies simultaneously

A. Use the cloze technique to model out loud, showing them how you use four cues (or "clues") concurrently. Try doing this once each day with a new sentence or paragraph. Make sure you have only one difficult word in each sentence. For example, here's one you might use:

> I like to *enlighten* students who have trouble reading a hard word.

To model your strategy with this particular sentence you might start by explaining to them that they are *not* to call out the word that you're going to have a problem with. Tell them you're going to pretend that you don't know the word so they can see how you solve the problem. The rule should be "Watch, don't talk." Also tell them to watch your act carefully, because when you're through, you're going to choose someone to come up and do the same act with a different word.

After you write the entire sentence on the board, begin your act by stumbling, "I like to..." Oh well, I'll just call this hard word "blank" and then I'll try reading the sentence again. "I like to blank students who have trouble reading a hard word." Hmmm! "I like to blank students who have trouble reading a hard word."

Then you can slowly wonder aloud, without looking directly at them: "Now don't anyone tell me, but I'm still wondering what word would fit in that blank? (Cautiously) It might mean something like 'help a student.' And it might have something to do with light because I see that word *light* in the middle of the word, So I think this word is en—*light*—en. Hmmm. Enlighten!

"I get it, so maybe this sentence means: I like to help students by shining a light, you know, to help them see or understand something more clearly."

Now, after reminding them of the "Watch, don't talk" rule, choose someone to act in the same way with this next sentence that you write on the board:

> That is not relevant to what we're talking about.

Now discuss a new word like *heave* in the context of the sentences or paragraphs in the story or information article they are about to read (or simply as a third activity):

> Three strong men began to heave the giant rock to the top.

Ask them to "prove" their understanding of the word in four ways:.

1. Graphophonic: "Prove that you're pronouncing the word correctly by showing me exactly how the letters and sounds go together."
2. Syntactic: "Prove that the word 'sounds right' in this sentence by changing just one word in the sentence. Change *heave* to *heaved* and read the new sentence out loud."

   > Three strong men began to heaved the giant rock to the top.

   > Which one sounds better? Why?

3. Semantic: "Prove that the word is the right word for the sentence by giving me a synonym (or a substitute) that would mean the same thing." (Students should eventually come up with something like *lift, push,* or *raise.*)
4. Schematic: "Prove the word is the right word for the sentence by telling about one of your own experiences with the word or someone else's experience with the word."

B. Closely guide their oral practice in predicting and checking predictions, pointing out the types of "clues" used or not used as each person reads. (Help them understand that this is the purpose of the lesson, and they will have the chance to read the entire selection without interruption.)

II. Intervene to increase their fluency and assist their comprehension

A. Provide fluency practice daily with very easy text. This will allow them to automatically use all four cues as they naturally do with easy listening experiences.
B. Provide fluent practice with predictable "patterned books" because of their built-in repetition of the four types of cues.
C. Provide comfortable echo, choral, and repeated reading experiences, again pointing out the types of "clues" that are available.
D. Enhance students' background knowledge and purpose before they read so that they can fluently use the three contextual cues (schematic, syntactic, semantic) as well as the graphophonic cues.

III. Sample Intervention that Can Enhance Their Schemas and Purposes

"Who do you think was braver—the astronauts who flew in tiny space modules to the moon in 1964 or the Columbus 'aquanauts' who sailed in tiny ships to America in 1492? Listen carefully to all of the steps we're going to use to prepare for our debate.

A. First I would like the students on the left side of the room to each find a small space on the board. When you have found that space, I would like you to write two important things you already know about the astronauts' flight to the moon.
B. At the same time, the students on the right side of the room will each write two important things they already know about the aquanauts' voyage to America.
C. Then the aquanaut team will gather new information by reading the article on (e.g., pages 35 to 42), and the astronaut team will gather new information by reading the article (e.g., on pages 43 to 50).
D. Next, the two teams will debate the question: "Who was braver—the crew of astronauts or the crew of aquanauts?"
E. And finally each of us, including myself, will write a page or so in our journal about the new things we learned from our reading, and a page or so about the new things we learned

from listening to the debate. Let the debate preparation begin..."

Activities for Building Schemas and Purposes with Younger Students*

Before they read on a particular topic, tease their interest and build their comprehension strategies with a cloze "guessing game." Each student tries to fill in the blanks in a selection of information text taken from a selection they are about to read from a book. Then they read about the topic, and finally, through memory and inferential thinking, they make any changes they wish on filling in the blank. (For some students, you may want to have them keep score on their correct blanks filled in the first time and then the second time after reading the actual article.)

Here's an example of a cloze article that can stimulate their interest in the topic:

A Strange Animal

__________ come in many sizes. The little ones weigh only two ounces and have wings that are only five inches from tip to tip. The largest __________ can have wings that are five __________ from tip to tip.

Although __________ spend a lot of time flying, they are very different from __________. Their bodies are covered with fur and not feathers. Their wings are covered with thin __________.

Many of them live on a diet of __________. Others feed on nectar from flowers, and some live on mice and other little __________. After they eat, they fly back to their home and __________ upside down to digest their food better.

Here's an example of another way to enhance both schemas and purposes with your students. Just tell them something like this: "I think monkeys are all alike. What do you think." After they share their ideas and after you have summarized them on the board, just say: "All right, read the story starting on page 39 and see if you can prove that I'm wrong about monkeys. I still think monkeys are all alike."

*In the next chapter you will find ways of compensating for the meanest "killer" of reading comprehension—the difficult and confusing text we often expect our students to read.

CHAPTER

6 The Sixth Myth of Reading

Myth 6, Part A: The Laziness Myth.

It's up to the student to learn to read well, regardless of text quality and difficulty. (If he'd just try harder, he'd succeed.)

Text Difficulty: The Oft Forgotten Factor in the Development and Assessment of Reading Comprehension

Have you noticed how some of us get so involved in counting the number of "correct answers" to our questions, we forget to assess the text quality as well as the students. The more difficult the text, of course, the more difficulty our students have in communicating with the author. We all know this to be true, but we often forget it, probably for good reason: After all, we were taught from early childhood days through the teens that it's our fault if we can't achieve at the level of our teachers' and parents' expectations. It was our fault if we couldn't hit the ball far enough to win the Little League game. It was our fault if we couldn't read at the fifth-grade level by the age of ten. And it was especially our fault if we couldn't safely drive the family car to Grandma's on an overcrowded, underdesigned freeway by age sixteen.

When we grew up and became teachers, we gratefully learned how to transform the concept of "our fault" to the delicious concept of "their fault." We learned to say things like, "He's ten years old and only reading at the first grade level!" or "She's not even writing at the phonemic level yet!" or perhaps "My principal's emotional awareness is level one on a ninety point scale!" As you can see, the word *level* can become a handy shield for us to carry with us at all times.

The Attempt to Assess Text Difficulty through Formulas

With gross judgments like those constantly entering through both ears and invading our brains, it's no wonder some of us educators have moved up to the next "level of labeling." I'm talking about our use of readability formulas for determining the "level of difficulty" for each book we encourage or require our students to read. Our purposes have been noble, but the danger of using formulas with people and the books they read, instead of people and the perfumes they wear is this: Formulas are designed for large groups of people and vast clusters of data. When you use formulas with people and their books you can become removed from the responsibility of treating every person in the group as in individual.

Let me give you an analogy between teachers and factory workers: This issue of determining levels of difficulty reminds me of an experience I had while consulting for an old-fashioned firm in Milwaukee. Back then, the Lewis Allis Motor Company was still manufacturing electric motors in the "good ol' way." They were losing money by the truckload and wanted to "modernize their procedures." I was hired as a consultant to create formulas for how much money the bosses should pay the piecework employees. (The factory workers got paid by the piece rather than by the hour.) By using formulas, the big bosses wouldn't have to think about each employee as an individual. They wouldn't have to pay expensive engineers to mosey around with a split-second stopwatch and observe each and every factory worker. Most of all, the big bosses wouldn't have to make uncomfortable, unpopular decisions about the difficulty, quality and speed of each employee's work—at a lathe, a stamping machine, a winding machine, or a grinder.

How Does this Relate to Teachers? Likewise, in reading education, we have created formulas for determining the difficulty level of reading materials that students will be reading. Consequently, teachers don't have to think as much about each individual in their classroom. More specifically, they don't have to think about the prior experiences and knowledge of each student and what books might be appropriate for each of them. If you translate "factory bosses" into "educators," and "pieceworkers" into "students," you can see that both educators and big bosses have been doing the same thing.

The most popular formula, the "Fry Formula," requires teachers and textbook publishers to think very little, indeed, about individual needs, learning styles, or reading interests. All we have to do in order to determine the reading difficulty of required reading is compute a tiny bit of "third grade level" arithmetic.

1. Select three 100-words from different parts of the book.
2. Count the total number of sentences in each 100-word passage and average those three numbers (which comes out to be, let's say, 5.6 sentences).
3. Now count the total number of syllables in each 100-word sample and average those three numbers (let's say 156 syllables).
4. On Fry's Graph (with the number of sentences on the vertical axis and the number of syllables on the horizontal axis) you now find the intersection between those two numbers (5.6 and 156). Presto! You immediately get an estimate of the difficulty level (fifth grade) for the whole book!

As you can see, this favorite formula, designed for publishers and teachers, and devised for estimating the reading comprehension level for a particular text, is based only on numerical factors, i.e., the number of syllables and the number of sentences. It's an ingenious formula, I suppose, but hardly an accurate one when it comes to real people reading real books.

Perhaps you have had the same experience I have had with formulas. I chose a book touted as "A high-interest, low vocabulary book, excellent for the 2nd grade reading level." Then I gave it to my potential drop-out student, age 15, thinking it would be perfect for him. The catch was that he became so frustrated he refused to "read" beyond the first two paragraphs of that "high-interest" story. Read the following text, for an example, one that's also rated as second-grade reading material.

> Arthur Finnington swung his lank legs out of bed and slumped on the edge in a stupor. He suddenly sat up straight. To himself he moaned, "Jeez, Saturday. My day for crimping some limeys."
>
> (So far we have 4 sentences and 45 syllables.)
>
> Inattentively, he plucked his togs from the earthen floor and covered his flimsy frame. His brain, sluggish from sleep, wanted to shut down, but willpower won out in the end. Arthur thought about Saturday last—a blimey good day crimping hard up journey-men, but too much trouble trying to keep them from leaving. This time he had to find other types, he resolved.

We have now added 4 more sentences and 87 more syllables; so we have a total of 8 sentences and 132 syllables. Using Fry's graph we find that we have a passage estimated to be at the second-grade level! Would you have considered that to be a reasonably accurate estimate?

I wouldn't either. So I decided to rewrite that passage, using my hard won knowledge about the experiential background of my 15-year-old "learning handicapped" student. This time he was able to read it all the way through with very little help. The revised story went like this:

> Arthur Finnington swung his thin legs out of bed and sat on the edge in a stupor. Suddenly he sat up straight. "Hey, it's Saturday!" he said to himself. "My day for making some money."
>
> Absentmindedly Arthur picked his clothes off the floor and began putting them on. His brain was sluggish from a good night's sleep, but he kept on trying to think anyway. He thought about last Saturday, a pretty good day selling homemade Popsicles, but too much trouble trying to keep them from melting. "This time it has to be something big," he mumbled.

Although this version was definitely easier, it was also rated on Fry's graph as at the "second grade level." Why? Because, like the first version, it also had 8 sentences and 132 syllables. Perhaps from this example, I've made you suspect the truth:

> No formula for text difficulty has been developed that takes into account the multifaceted nature of reading comprehension. No formula that I know of, and there are many in existence, takes into account the degree to which a student will have trouble making use of her limited prior knowledge in order to understand the author. No formula takes into account the degree to which she might be restrained by text obscurity from making good use of her decoding and comprehension strategies. In short, no readability formula (that I know of) is capable of assessing unsuitable text.

To put it another way, formulas assess reading products such as the number of syllables and sentences or, with some formulas, the recognition of a specified list of words. Formulas are not suitable, though, for assessing reading *processes.* An experienced teacher or parent who has observed a particular student reading a variety of texts, of various difficulties, is a much better "assessor" than a mathematical readability formula.

Developing Reading Comprehension Despite Unclear Incoherent Text

Here's a question: Is clear, coherent, compatible text really that important to students' success in understanding the author's message? Let's find out by examining the conclusions determined from four research studies done by a group of five researchers. (These studies by McKeown, Beck, Sinatra, Loxterman, and Gromell are described more fully in Part B.)

The 1989 textbook study. The researchers found that much of the information in textbooks is so abbreviated, out of context, and abstracted, that readers can't build vivid meanings or images in their minds. Authors and publishers, they found, often assume too much prior knowledge and experiences on the part of the readers.

The 1990 study of readers. By interviewing fifth-grade readers before they studied the colonial period in the United States, the researchers found that most of them had only vague and inaccurate prior knowledge of this period of history. Did this mean the textbook selections in the 1989 study were too difficult and incompatible? Or did this mean that the teachers had not provided enough knowledge and schema development before the students had been asked to read the text?

The 1991 Revised-Text Study. The researchers rewrote the text so that facts were now related to each other, the writing was more clear, and it didn't require as much prior knowledge. As a result, reading comprehension was much better for the revision group than the control group who read the original "bad text." But what if the teachers had spent more time developing prior knowledge and schemas? Wouldn't the control students' comprehension have been just as good?

The 1992 Combined Study. This time, the researchers had one group use the revised text and one group use the original bad text. But both groups were given the same interesting information that would enhance their schemas and enlarge their prior knowledge. Did such enhancement make up for the bad text, and, therefore, did the groups do equally well on comprehension? Not so. The group that had both schema enhancement and well-written text were the clear winners.

A Final Thought on the Relationship between Text Difficulty and Reading Comprehension

So now we're ready to answer the original question: Is clear, coherent, compatible text really that important to students' success in understanding the author's message? Probably the word *important* is not the word we're looking for. The word *crucial* or *consequential* would describe the situation more precisely.

> Even though our goals and procedures as reading teachers are designed to model and assist reading comprehension, do we not sabotage both our goals and means by paying too little attention to the quality and confusion of the text we provide for PRACTICE?

Increasing Text Comprehension without Worshiping Main Ideas

Because of a very long tradition, and because of our desire to make unsuitable text more understandable to our students, many of us educators have tried to help them "search for the main ideas." We have reinforced this strategy, I suppose, by telling each other that finding the main ideas is the only way for a student to really understand the author, particularly an incoherent one.

Because of another tradition, some of us have told our students that the main idea can be found in the "topic sentence" of each paragraph. And to oversimplify even more, we've told them "the topic sentence is usually the first sentence in the paragraph." We kind of whisper that last bit of advice in their ear, so they'll know we're on their side in this confusing world of real language. It might be better, perhaps, to study the research on "finding main ideas." Here's a brief summary of the research.

1. At best, only one paragraph in eight contains a topic sentence.
2. Main ideas are very difficult for most students to find.
3. Educators don't and can't agree on the nature of main ideas and "what to look for."

My attempt to help inexperienced readers find the author's meaning has gradually made me realize that searching for main ideas can quickly turn into a mindless way of communicating with another human being. Even when I'm reading nonfiction, rather than fiction, I find that main ideas are rarely tucked neatly into one little sentence. They are much more often dispersed, like perfume, throughout the entire section or chapter—or book for that matter!

> Expecting to find the author's main idea in one sentence or paragraph is like expecting to find the theme of an entire symphony in one measure, or to find the total essence of a poem in its title.

Besides, no published author I know of is full of that many main ideas! If any self-respecting author did have that many, she or he wouldn't do anything so unnatural as to squeeze each main idea into a tiny little topic sentence. If you truly want your students to search for meaning, you may want to ask not for "the main idea" but for something more personal such as: "What did the author make you feel inside as you read that last part?" or "Did you learn something that will be useful to you in your own life?" or "What do you think the author (or character really believes about this? Do you agree with the author (or character)? Why (or why not)?"

In What Other Ways Can Teachers Compensate for Confusing Text?

Let me just mention a few general ways for now, with more specific ways coming up later:

1. Use the writing mode to help students learn how to clarify their own writing and the writing of an author.
2. You can also substitute trade books for textbooks (like those listed in Part E).
3. You can rewrite the text yourself, or rewrite it with your student, or have your gifted students rewrite it for peers who are having trouble reading it, as shown in Part E.
4. In addition, you can use your professional power to write constructive critical letters to textbook and trade book publishers.
5. What is even more important, you can teach your students how to monitor their own degree of understanding, so they can determine the specific help they need. (This is demonstrated for you in Part E.)

Myth 6, Part B: Research That Refutes the Sixth Myth of Reading.

A Review of Reading Comprehension Research

Dole, J. A., Duffy, G. G., Roehler, L. R., Pearson, P. D. (1991). Moving from the old to the new: Research on reading comprehension instruction. *Review of Educational Research, 61,* 2, 239–264.

One of their Conclusions: "Even expert readers can be reduced to novices when presented with obscure or ambiguous texts" (p. 241).

A Study on Clarifying Difficult Text through Story Maps

Beck, I. L., Omanson, R. C., McKeown, M. G. (1982). An instructional redesign of reading lessons: Effects on comprehension. *Reading Research Quarterly, 17,* 4, 462–481.

Conclusions

1. "Comprehension of single texts can be enhanced by a careful structuring of the lesson elements surrounding the story text" (p. 478).
2. A successful text-conscious lesson plan can assist students to comprehend both easy and difficult text.
3. A very important element in a text-conscious lesson plan is that of determining ahead of time the "central" concepts and information you wish the student to comprehend before, during, and after they have read both the easy and difficult portions of the text.
4. Emphasizing central concepts and information before, during and after reading together is an essential procedure in clarifying difficult text and allowing students to participate in creating a summarizing story map.

Four Studies on the Importance of Well-Written Text for Productive Reading Practice

Study 1: Beck, I. L., McKeown, M. G., & Gromoll, E. W. (1989). Learning from social studies texts. *Cognition and Instruction,* 6, 99–158.

Conclusions

1. Much of the information in the children's textbooks was abbreviated, detached, and abstracted so much, the readers often

couldn't build vivid images in their minds. The textbook information on the U.S. colonial period, for instance, was being presented to fifth graders as isolated, unrelated facts and ideas. Details and examples were often missing.

2. The authors seemed to assume far too much prior knowledge on the part of their readers. This, of course, made it very difficult for students to fill in the empty slots with their own inferences.

Study 2: McKeown, M. G., & Beck, I. L. (1990). The assessment and characterization of young learner's knowledge of a topic in history. *American Educational Research Journal,* 27, 688–726

Procedures. The researchers interviewed fifth graders just before they were to study the revolutionary period of U.S. history. They examined two major erroneous assumptions the textbook authors had made: (1) the children would already understand the role of England in the colonists' struggle for independence, (2) they would already understand the concept of representative government.

Results of Interviews

1. Many children were familiar, but only in a general sense, with this historical period.
2. The vast majority of the children had ideas that were vague and inaccurate.
3. The vast majority did not understand the role of England in the colonists' struggle for independence.
4. The vast majority did not understand the concept of representative government.

Study 3: Beck, I.L., McKeown, M.G., Sinatra, G.M., & Loxterman, J.A. (1991). Revising social studies text from a text-processing perspective: Evidence of improved comprehensibility. *Reading Research Quarterly, 26,* 252–276.

Procedure: The researchers rewrote the text so that it was clear and coherent: The facts were now related to each other and didn't require as much prior knowledge as the original text. Why? Because the necessary details and "word-pictures" were inserted in the revised text.

Conclusion: Reading comprehension was much better for the revision group than the control group that read the original difficult text.

Study 4: McKeown, M. G., Beck, I. L., Sinatra, G. M., & Loxterman, J. A. (1992). The contribution of prior knowledge and coherent text to comprehension. *Reading Research Quarterly, 27,* 79–93.

Procedures: This time, the researchers had one group use the revised text and one group use the original bad text. But both groups were given the same interesting information that would enhance and enlarge their prior knowledge.

Conclusions

1. Schema enhancement did not completely make up for the confusing text.
2. The group that had both schema enhancement and well-written text did the best in understanding the author.
3. The students who had to read bad text, judging from the previous three studies, would have done even more poorly if they hadn't been provided with background knowledge and schema enhancement.

Studies Showing Problems Involved in Searching for Main Ideas

Study 5: Donlan, D. (1980). Locating main ideas in history textbooks. *Journal of Reading, 24,* 135–140.

Conclusion: Only one in every eight paragraphs had a topic sentence.

Study 6: Cunningham, J. W., & Moore, D. W. (1986). The confused world of main idea. In J. F. Baumann (Ed.), *Teaching main idea comprehension* (pp.1–17). Newark, DE: International Reading Association.

Conclusion: There are at least nine notions among educators of what a main idea really is: gist, interpretation, key word, selective summary, theme, title, topic, topic issue, topic sentence.

Study 7: Duffelmeyer, F. A. & Duffelmeyer, B. B. (1987). Main idea questions on informal reading inventories. *Reading Teacher, 41,* 162–166.

Conclusion: Many educators think that main ideas are nothing more than topics.

Comment: Do we really think we can compensate for incoherent, incompatible authors by searching for something so mythical and inadequate as their main ideas?

Research Review Showing the Importance of Writing to Reading

Quian, G. (1990, November). *Review of the interactive model: Reconsideration of reading and writing relationship.* Paper presented at the annual meeting of the College Reading Association, Nashville, TN.

Conclusion: Writing experiences can have a positive effect on students' reading comprehension and their critical thinking abilities.

Myth 6, Part C: Factual Case Study Illustrating Reading Problems That May Arise from the Belief that It's up to the Student to Learn to Read Well, regardless of Text Quality and Difficulty. Failure to Provide Clear and Compatible Text for Students' Reading Practice

Patrick the Failure—Maybe

Patrick was scheduled to flunk second grade in five weeks because of his grades in reading. His parents displayed their disapproval over the phone and in person. Patrick's teacher was sympathetic but patiently showed them the daily test scores on Patrick's reading assignments. The scores ranged from 20% to 60%, a depressing bit of news for his parents. His teacher, Mrs. Hoskins, was also depressed because she had "tried so hard to get him up to third-grade level." She called me at my university office and asked if I would "test him out and find out what he was doing wrong."

I met Patrick in early April, with only seven weeks to go before "flunk time." I was not exactly optimistic as I plunged into the morass of self-deprecation, guilt, and depression that Patrick exhibited. These emotions were demonstrated by his halting speech, twitchy facial expressions, and skittish body language. With more than a little reluctance I listened to him read, "Wrecking a Building," the selection his teacher had asked him to read to us.

You might like to imagine yourself in the shoes of this struggling eight-year-old second grader as you read this rather unclear, incoherent, and incompatible piece of information. It is a sunless, drizzly day in Portland, Oregon, and you are about to read it "cold" (as your teacher had just asked you to do it). There was no discussion of your prior knowledge on the topic; no chance to visualize what the article was about; and no check on your specific concepts or notions about buildings, about wrecking something, about "engineers," crowbars, "clamshells," bulldozers, or cranes.

Wrecking a Building

Wreckers get paid for knocking down buildings. Before any wrecking can begin, the engineers look at the plans of the building and choose equipment for the wreckers. Sometimes they make plans for saving parts of the buildings.

Usually they put up a fence made of doors removed from the building to keep people safe. They block off the sidewalk with safety signs, and turn off the electricity, gas, and water.

They bring down the building with crowbars or a clamshell or a ball. The crane operator moves the long beam attached to the high mast that guides the ball swinging at the end of the cable. When a large wall falls it makes a lot of noise.

The clamshell operator makes the jaws take hold of the top of a wall or a beam. He makes the jaws lift, pulling the wall apart or the beam out, and the smashed and broken parts are loaded into the trucks. Bulldozers which usually clear land and move soil and lift boulders can be used for scooping up the rest of the building. Once the ground is cleared, the builders can come in.

How did you feel as you read this (as a second grader)? Any anxieties or confusion? Patrick felt both. He must have felt like a potential visitor in Hades, judging from the slumped position in his chair, his "begging-for-mercy glance" toward his teacher, and his deep sighs exhaled every three to five words.

After his teacher quickly "finished with him" (by pronouncing every word he couldn't decode), she stood off at the side and watched the two of us "go through the story again." I took a very deep breath and nervously attempted to demonstrate to Mrs. Hoskins how she could provide Patrick with the mercy he deserved. First, for his sake and mine, I tried to put him at ease by saying: "The person who wrote this story didn't know how to write very well, did he?"

(We were sitting side by side, at a far back corner of the classroom, looking at the same pages.)

This time he gave a small sigh of relief instead of despair. He actually smiled as he said in a stage whisper, "No way, Ho-zay." His teacher smiled encouragement at him, and that seemed to make him feel all the better. (Her parent aide was working with the rest of the class while Mrs. Hoskins observed.) It was a pleasure to see her so eager to help Patrick succeed.

Next I told Patrick what was really happening in this "story" about wreckers, using words he could relate to and amateur descriptions that I sketched on a small chalkboard. This seemed to help him understand, or perhaps remember, what all those gigantic and expensive tools did to assist the wreckers: the bulldozer, the clamshell, the crane, and so on.

After I told the story that way, I read it aloud to him while he followed along by my side. We went slowly, using the echo method: I would read a sentence to him and then listen to his echoed rendition of the same sentence. (At times I had to break up a sentence into phrases that he could echo.) And then, after each sentence, I asked him what he saw in his mind? What did he hear? What did he feel?

After the first two paragraphs, he sat up a bit, appearing to have found a tiny new feeling of energy inside him. Hopefully this was a sign that he might eventually realize that reading might be an "okay thing." After a discussion of what he had learned from the first paragraph, we read the same paragraph together in choral fashion—a reasonably successful duet that caused the teacher to smile at both of us this time.

On the next day, we reviewed what he had learned about the crane, bulldozer, clamshell, wrecking ball, and the trucks that hauled the wreckage away. Then we rolled up our sleeves, literally, at my invitation and completely rewrote the first paragraph. We were observed by the teacher but from a greater distance, and in only a few minutes we were smiling and having fun. It was obvious to me that he did not want to be "a failure" and was eager to get some relief from his burden.

We fearlessly changed the author's words to easier synonyms and inserted many missing details. Gradually this process evolved from dual problem solving into dictation from Patrick to me. At his wish I was partially transformed from a teacher into a menial hack whose printing was required more than his advice. The problem solving and dictation were followed by intense practicing of the new version. And that was the end of our second session. But before I tell you about the third and last day, here's our typed copy of our coauthored revision.

> ***How the Wreckers Knock Down a Building***
>
> Some people get paid lots of money for knocking down buildings. Those people are called wreckers. Maybe you have heard about car wreckers, who take cars apart that no one wants anymore. Building wreckers do the same thing with old buildings that no one wants anymore.
>
> Before any building can be knocked down, the wreckers have to put up a huge fence around the building. This keeps people from getting hurt from falling bricks or stone or lumber. The wreckers also put up signs on the fence that say, "Danger. Wreckers are knocking down this building. Stay outside the fence."

As you can see, we made the original paragraph "stick together" better by picturing the wreckers getting ready to knock down a building. We also added some suspense by describing the warning sign. At the same time we made the original paragraph more coherent by changing one paragraph into two—one on what wreckers do for a living and one on how they get ready for the big event.

On our third and last day together, we practiced reading the two new paragraphs. Patrick found it quite easy to read the paragraphs he had "revised" with me. For a celebration he read them to his teacher who, of course, beamed even brighter than I did.

Before I left, his teacher and I made plans for how the rest of the informational story could be revised and learned in the same way, with the teacher or teacher aide as his reading partner and coauthor. We also planned ways of finding other texts for Patrick that would be more relevant and interesting and, of course, much more "clear, coherent, and compatible."

Patrick and his parents, along with the intensive help from Mrs. Hoskins and two parent aides, did the rest. And yes—not that this always happens—he actually did fail! (He failed to flunk second grade.)

Myth 6, Part D: Quick Assessment Devices for Determining Reading Problems that May Have Developed because of the Belief that It's Up to the Student to Learn to Read Well, Regardless of Text Quality and Difficulty.

Self-Evaluation Checklist for Teachers

______ 1. I feel that my students are largely responsible for their own learning and for their motivation to learn how to read well.

______ 2. I spend very little time preparing my students to read a particular story or information piece, because I want them to have more time for actual reading.

______ 3. I sometimes revise reading selections for those students who find the text unclear, disjointed, or poorly organized.

______ 4. For clarifying the meaning of a writer's text, I nearly always rely on teaching students how to find the main ideas.

______ 5. For teaching about main ideas I usually have them read the topic sentence in each paragraph.

______ 6. In teaching a student how to read well, the clarity of the text is not as important as the student's sheer hard work.

______ 7. I usually prepare for reading assignments by determining the most important concepts my students will face and how I can explain them before they read.

______ 8. Probably my most frequent question for my students is "What is the main idea in that paragraph (or page)?"

______ 9. While I read with a student (or students), I like to ask questions that are personally meaningful or relevant like, "Did you learn something that will be useful to you in your own life?" or "Do you believe Mr. Smith was right? Why or Why not?"

______ 10. I don't think it's right for my students to criticize an author's writing for what they think is his lack of clarity!

______ 11. I like to use graphic illustrations, such as story maps, for helping my students summarize the characters, ideas, conflicts, or sequences.

______ 12. Most textbooks are too difficult for students because they don't give enough examples, supporting details, or clear descriptions.*

Probable Isolated Symptoms of Chronic Exposure to Difficult Text (for Ages 8 and over with English or Another First Language)

Student's Name: ______ Date: ______ Total: ______ out of 7

______ 1. Comprehension seems good when reading aloud (to a solitary friendly adult) most fiction and nonfiction designed for ages 5 to 7, but comprehension seems poor when reading most fiction and nonfiction designed for his own age (isolation of comprehension abilities from text difficulties).

______ 2. Fluent (flowing) reading aloud (to a solitary friendly adult) of fiction and nonfiction designed for ages 5 to 7, but nonfluent reading aloud (to a solitary friendly adult) of most fiction and nonfiction designed for his own age (isolation of fluency and comprehension).

______ 3. Comprehension usually good when listening to fiction and nonfiction designed for his own age and two years beyond his age (isolation of reading comprehension from listening comprehension).

______ 4. Attitude toward reading usually poor, but attitude toward school similar to attitude of your grade-level students (isolation of reading attitude from school attitude).

______ 5. Phonological awareness tasks, including phoneme segmentation, phoneme blending, syllable beats, rhyming, alliteration, and intonation variations in speech handled as well as your grade-level students (isolation of phonological difficulties from text difficulties).

*A perfect score for your awareness of the Importance of Text Difficulty to Reading Comprehension is "5" if you chose only #3, #7, #9, #11, and #12.

______ 6. Phonic awareness tasks, including common blends, digraphs, phonograms, vowel patterns, and connection of rimes and onsets, handled as well as your grade-level students (isolation of phonics difficulties from text difficulties).

______ 7. Morpheme and syntax awareness tasks (while speaking or writing), including syllable division, affixes, roots, intonation, and word order, are handled as well as your grade-level students (isolation of morpheme and syntax difficulties from text difficulties).

Myth 6, Part E: Positive Intervention Procedures Designed to Help Students Whose Teachers and Parents Have Believed that It's Up to the Student to Learn to Read Well, Regardless of Text Quality and Difficulty.

Step One: Instead of requiring all of your students to read textbook assignments, provide at least some of them with readable trade books about the same textbook topics. See the following list for sources of annotated lists of trade books.

Early Childhood through Middle School Sources of English Text that Can Substitute for Difficult Textbook Information

1. *Notable Children's Trade Books in the Field of Social Studies.* Annual list obtained from Children's Book Council, 67 Irving Place, New York, NY 10003. Also appears in every April/May issue of *Social Education.*
2. *Outstanding Science Trade Books for Children.* Published in every March issue of *Science and Children.* (Also available from Children's Book Council (address above).
3. *Book Links,* a bimonthly magazine containing annotations of trade books related to topics and themes, such as Families, Deserts, and so on. A perfect source for teachers using integrated themes.
4. *Children's Books,* a department appearing each month in *The Reading Teacher.* This department frequently provides a special annotated list of new social studies, humanities, and science

trade books, both fiction and nonfiction, available for students from preschool through middle school.

5. *Teacher's Choices*, an annual list of outstanding trade books, fiction and nonfiction, that teachers find to be exceptionally useful for cross-subject programs. This list can be obtained with a 9" × 12" self-addressed, two-stamp envelope from International Reading Association, P.O. Box 8139, Newark, DE 19714. *Teacher's Choices* is also available in the November issues of *The Reading Teacher.*
6. Here is another fine source for locating fiction and nonfiction trade books: Multicultural Literature for Children and Young Adults, Volume Two, by Ginny Moore Kruse, Kathleeen T. Horning, and Megan Schliesman. This can be obtained from the Cooperative Children's Book Center, School of Education, University of Wisconsin-Madison. The phone number is 608-263-3720 and the fax is 608-262-4933.

> With at least 30,000 new school-age trade books being published each decade, there is very little reason for teachers and administrators to have their students stumbling along with no more motivation than to "get through the textbook assignment." Nor is there any reason to have them keep on practicing their inferior reading strategies like no-shows and false substitutes just to get through the textbook assignment. And there's definitely no reason for young readers to develop poor attitudes toward the act of reading because of unclear, incoherent, abstract, incompatible text.

Step Two: Teach your students how to recognize noncommunicative writing through monitoring their own reading comprehension. Comprehension monitoring is the process of being your own coach. A track coach, for instance, teaches his or her apprentices to ask questions of themselves, like these:

1. "What's my *goal* for the next pole vault?"
2. "How can I *change* my performance to meet that goal?"
3. "How can I *concentrate* better on my sequence of moves?"
4. "What *information* do I need that will help me do better?"

In the same way, the teacher of reading can model reading comprehension behavior by asking herself or himself similar questions. (Modify these questions to fit your students.) Just address them aloud to yourself in a way your students will understand):

1. Should I skim this one to see if I really want to spend time reading it?
2. What is my goal for reading this? Am I keeping my goal in mind or am I just covering the pages?
3. Should I read this just for the story (or information) or will I enjoy it more if I pay more attention to the characters, the author's humor, logic, or biases?
4. How can I picture the events (or steps) the author wants me to follow?
5. What information is missing or confusing that makes me not understand?

A Learning Activity on Monitoring Progress with Difficult Text

The teacher selects several pieces of difficult text to use over a week's time. Then she models each of the five self-questions above with each selection. Some selections you choose will allow you to ask all five questions; some only two or three.

For your first one you may wish to use this humorous story:

Make sure you do this activity with an overhead projector, so that you're all looking at the same copy. Keep them from reading ahead by sliding down a 5 × 8 card one or two lines at a time. The following selection will allow you to ask all five questions. Right after the story about "Cars" a script follows for your use. For your other selections, I recommend making a script until you're used to modeling this way.

Cars Can Be Very Dangerous

Whether you drive a car or just ride in a car, there are things you should learn about safety. I'm sure you have been told, while driving with your mother, not to stick your arm out of the car window. You know why, don't you? Because some dreadful person will immediately drive by and knock it off!

Just knock it clean off!! Nothing left but a shoulder! Or at least, that's what I pictured at the age of five, every time my mother told me not to stick my arm out of the car window.

But Mom," I would say, "you stick your arm out all the time."

And she'd always say, "I'm just signaling a left turn."

Since I didn't understand my right from my left until I was ten years old, I didn't catch her meaning. And when she used the word *signaling,* all I could think of was my older brother Billy who learned in the Boy Scouts how to signal with red flags made of cloth and sticks. He could signal difficult things like A or B or C. In fact, he could even signal every letter in my name, which used to be John, but I changed it to Jonathan Livingston Seagull and he couldn't do it anymore.

So anyway, I would always say to Mom, "Why don't you signal with Billy's red flags?" And she'd always look in the rearview mirror and frown at me and say, "I think you've lost all your marbles."

After she said that, I would become more confused than ever. I didn't know what the word *left* meant. I didn't know why my mother didn't take my good advice and use those red flags for signaling. And I never could figure out how I could have lost all my marbles, when I clearly had all thirty-three of them in my pocket. I had just counted them in the car for the seventh time in a row.

"Which pocket, right or left?" my brother Billy would ask me. And with considerable irritation, I would respond, "This one!" pointing to the bulging bumpiness that lay right under my thigh-length pants.

And Billy would say, "That's the right pocket."

Now then—I told you I didn't know my right from my left—right? What I didn't tell you was this: I also didn't know the word *right* has two meanings: the opposite of *left* and the opposite of *wrong.*

So I would now ask my mother, "Is this the right one, Mom?"

And she would say sweetly, "I can't tell if it's the right one or the wrong one."

Well, I got so frustrated with all that left and right jazz! When they finally let me out of the car, I was steaming. I was furious. And I slammed the door with all my five-year-old might!

Right on my thumb!!

My right one, my left one, whatever!!!

The really important thing is, I learned an awesome lot about safety when it comes to cars. And so, I'm just passing on to you everything I learned, as well as everything I didn't learn.

Please be careful about your arms and your thumbs. As my mother always told me, "You can only grow them once."

One Way to Model the Five Questions with "Cars Can Be Dangerous"

1. (First Paragraph) I'm going to read a little bit of this to myself to see if I really want to read it all. The title is: "Cars can be very dangerous." That sounds important, so I'll read a little more. "Whether you drive a car or just ride in a car, there are things you should learn about safety." Okay, now I know this is going to be about staying safe when you're riding in a car. I'll read some more and see if I need to read the rest of it. "I'm sure you have been told, while driving with your mother, not to stick your arm out of the car window. You know why, don't you? Because some dreadful person will immediately drive by and knock it off." Wow, this might be fun to read. I like the funny way the author was exaggerating the problem. I think I'll read the whole thing. But first, let me think some more. Why do I want to read it? (What's my goal?) I want to read it to find out how I can be safe in a car, and I want to read it to see how funny this story is going to be.

2. "Just knock it clean off. Nothing left but a shoulder. Or at least, that's what I pictured at the age of five, every time my mother told me not to stick my arm out of the window." Now I know I'm going to enjoy reading the rest of this. I can tell it's going to be a real story and not just about safety. Should I read this just to see what happens, or should I also enjoy the way the author writes the story? I know! I'll do both!!

3. "'But Mom,'" I would say, "'you stick your arm out all the time!'" Ha! That's what I always *said* to *my* mother.

4. And she'd always say, "I'm just signaling a left turn." Just what my mother said—because we had a very old car without turn signals that blinked in back of the car and warned people behind us that we were going to turn. This story must be about a boy living many years ago. I can just picture him sitting in the back seat, and his mother is sitting in the driver's seat. I wonder if anyone else was in the car. I wonder what style of clothes they're wearing.

5. "Since I didn't understand my right from my left until I was ten years old, I didn't catch her meaning. And when she used the word *signaling,* all I could think of was my older brother Billy who learned in the Boy Scouts how to signal with red flags made of cloth and sticks." Yeah, I used those in the Girl Scouts. "He could signal difficult things like A or B or C. In fact, he could even signal every letter in my name, which used to be John, until I changed it to Jonathan Livingston Seagull." Ha! I read that book too.

6. "So anyway," I would say to Mom, "Why don't you signal with Billy's red flags?" And she'd look in the rear view mirror and frown at me and say, "I think you've lost all your marbles." Hmm. I've forgotten what that means. Oh yes, it's a friendly joke that means I've lost my brain and I'm not thinking clearly.

7. "After she said that, I'd always be more confused than ever. I didn't know what the word *left* meant. I didn't know why my mother didn't take my good advice and use those red flags for signaling. And I never could figure out how I could have lost all my marbles, when I clearly had all thirty-three of them in my pocket. I had just counted them for the seventh time in a row."

8. "I would say loudly to my mother. 'I've got my marbles in my pocket!' And my brother Billy, sitting much too closely to me, would say something silly like, 'Which pocket, right or left?' And with considerable irritation, I would respond, 'This one!' pointing to the bulging bumpiness that lay right under my thigh-length pants." Hmm. I can sort of picture that. He was wearing short pants and one of his front pockets was stuffed with thirty-three marbles.

9. "And Billy would say, 'That's the right pocket.'"

10. "Now then—I told you I didn't know my right from my left—right? What I didn't tell you was this: I also didn't know the word *right* has two meanings: the opposite of *left* and the opposite of *wrong*."

11. "Well, I got so frustrated with all that left and right jazz! When they finally let me out of the car, I slammed the door with all my five-year-old might!"

12. "Right on my thumb!!"

13. "My right one, my left one, whatever!!!"

14. "The really important thing is, I learned an awesome lot about safety when it comes to cars. And so, I'm just passing on to you everything I learned, as well as everything I didn't learn."

15. "Here's my advice to you. Please be careful about your arms and your thumbs. As my mother always told me, 'You can only grow them once.'"

When you finish reading the story and modeling for them, you might decide to help them remember some of the things you modeled for them by immediately putting up a chart that looks something like this:

How You Can Be Your Own Coach When You Read

Ask yourself these questions:

1. Why do I want to read this? I'll read the first part to see why.
3. What questions do I want to answer by reading it?
4. How can I picture in my mind what the author is telling me?
5. Which parts am I enjoying the most: The Action? Characters? Ideas?
6. What words or ideas are confusing me? I'll ask someone to help me.

Step Three: Teach them through modeling how to write in such a way that their story or message is clear, detailed enough, and sticks together like Oreo Cookies™. By learning how to write better, they can learn how to read better and to better monitor or coach their own reading (See Part B, Research).

Let me suggest that you model for your students one or two writing decisions each day, followed that same day by having them imitate your modeling. Here's a modeling schedule that may work well for you:

Monday: Plan aloud something you're going to write yourself, jotting down very brief notes on large butcher paper as you plan.

1. Decide how to please yourself by writing about an event, a person, or a place that interests you, e.g., "I liked my stay in Paris so much, I think I'll celebrate by writing a story about one of my adventures there, the one where I was accused by the police for stealing something I saw a shoplifter steal."
2. Then decide (in front of them) whether you want to write it as fiction or nonfiction. "I'll write it as a fiction story—maybe a pretend newspaper story that I'll send to my sister. That way I can make it even more interesting by exaggerating things that happened."
3. Now let them jot down their own notes on (1) and (2). (either by themselves or with a partner, depending on how they like to write).

Tuesday:

1. Think aloud about one of these: Your nonfiction subject or your fictional story. Jot down details on your butcher paper "plan sheet."

2. Think aloud about who your audience will be (and why you think they will be the most interested in reading it).
3. After you finish modeling (1) & (2) for them, let them do the same with a partner. That way each partner can start his or her plan sheet.

Wednesday: Think aloud about your fictional characters or about the real people in your nonfictional writing. Jot notes on your large plan sheet.

Thursday: Think aloud about conflicts you can insert in your writing to make your writing more spicy and interesting. Decide whether you want conflicts between people, or between people and nature, or within yourself.

Friday: Read to them the first two paragraphs or so of your own writing. Let them write their own two or more paragraphs.

Plans for Future (A): Write and help each other write each day till finished. Revise yours in front of them. Let them revise theirs with help of a partner. Edit and help each other edit until the standards set up by the entire group are met:

1. Each sentence is clear and easy to understand.
2. Each action is easy to see and hear in your mind..
3. Each character is easy to see and hear.

Plans for Future (B): Use the same process in reverse by reading a selection together and noticing how the author was sometimes unclear or confusing. Decide together how you could fix the writing so that you and others would understand it better.*

*Perhaps you noticed how we've been moving from cognitive aspects of learning to read to more emotional aspects of learning to read. In the final chapter, Chapter 7, you and I can concentrate on the role of emotions, attitudes, and motivations in the processes of reading and learning to read.

CHAPTER

7 The Seventh Myth of Reading

Myth 7, Part A: Reading and Learning to Read Is Much More Cognitive Than Motivational.

Before we get into the seventh myth of reading, let's make sure we both use the same definition of motivation. In this chapter, motivation will refer to being moved into action or thought by:

1. The sheer pleasure of learning
2. The drive for achievement
3. The students' interest in certain topics
4. The incentives in the learning environment arranged by the teacher
5. The basic needs for safety, belonging, self-esteem, and self-actualization

The motivation to read is derived additionally from memories of emotions associated with prior reading, e.g., joy, success, excitement, and tranquility. The motivation not to read may be derived from such memories as anxiety, self-disgust, failure, and angry frustration associated with prior reading.

Research described later in Part B indicates that positive motivations are vital to the process of learning to read well and to the feeling of satisfaction derived from reading. What does this mean for you, the teacher? Because the teacher is the orchestra leader, you're the chosen one to help them motivate themselves to create beautiful music (or beautiful reading in this case). As orchestra leader, of course, it's your responsibility to know the music very well. In the case of reading it's your responsibility to know other things very well, such as:

1. Those contrasting teaching procedures that lead to intrinsic or extrinsic motivation to read, and those procedures that lead to lack of motivation or the antimotivation to read.

2. Those contrasting teaching procedures that either cause or alleviate the stress and anxiety of students in the process of learning to read well.

Contrasting Teaching Procedures That Lead to Intrinsic Motivation, Extrinsic Motivation, or Lack of Motivation for Reading

To help you imagine those three forms of teaching, I'll depict first a teacher who inspires effective intrinsic motivation for reading and learning to read; second, a teacher who provides effective extrinsic motivation for reading and learning to read; and third, a teacher who utilizes antimotivational procedures. In each of the following cases the students' motivations are significantly influenced by the teacher's belief or lack of belief in the seventh myth of reading.

A Teacher Who Inspired Intrinsic Motivation for Reading

Ray Lubway was my older and more experienced team-teacher at the University of Chicago Laboratory School (founded by John Dewey before Ray and I were born). Ray Lubway was a lithe dancer of a man, with a slight build and brown eyes that flashed with pleasure whenever his students caught on to an idea, and especially when they created their own ideas. It was his belief that learning is a cognitive process, but even more so, a motivational process, although the processes continuously interact.

Learning to read and write better were considered by him to be crucial prerequisites to success and pleasure—in school, out of school, and after schooling. But to Ray, it was the variety of ways people learn to read and write better that made a difference to his students. The foremost form of variety was to teach in such a way that each student felt she or he was going to survive daily, tomorrow, and well into the future. (If I may be facetious, there's something warm and cozy about the feelings of safety and survival, isn't there? They're perhaps the most basic kind of feelings, the ones that start the heavy, three-holed learning ball rolling toward the head pin and not the gutter.)

John Holt demonstrated this for teachers many years ago in his book *The Way It's S'pose' to Be*. In this book, Holt, who was the teacher as well as the author, portrayed student after student who perceived the educational situation from the survival point of view. The kids who seemed to be surviving the best were those who believed in themselves. Al Siebert, author of *The Survival Personality,* describes the same perceptions of adults who survived in World War II by believing in themselves.

And this was also the way Ray Lubway perceived his students. More than anything else, Ray wanted his nine- and ten-year-olds to believe in themselves. He wanted them to read well, of course, but not just so they could survive or avoid the loss of respect from elders and peers. He wanted them to become intrinsically motivated to read for sheer pleasure, for information vital to their own purposes, and for that wonderful, personal feeling of success.

> Intrinsic motivation is private—something secret inside each of us, something that says, "Yes, what I'm doing right now is what I can and want to do. It's fun, it's interesting, it's challenging, it's not boring or babyish, and I can do it." Intrinsic motivation refers to the essence of what you feel you're gaining as you read.

Lubway's Spur to Intrinsic Motivation through Drama and Story Creation

Lubway used "drama" and "story creation" as two of the most important means for inspiring intrinsic motivation. Of course, story creation is a major form that authors use to produce what readers eventually read. And so, as Merlin did with King Arthur, Lubway often led his students backward, so to speak. Instead of always presenting them with high quality adult-written stories to read, he helped his students invent their own stories and tape record them as a community enterprise. This totally spontaneous event proceeded in a very inventive way:

TEACHER: Okay, let's try this: Once upon a time there was a terrible storm in the land called Mud. (Why do you think the people called it Mud?)

ALBERT: Ooh, I know. It was called Mud because it rained a whole lot every single day—and night too.

TEACHER: Yes, and so one day it rained so much, the strong, handsome, and dark King of Mud came out of his castle and spoke to all the people—with a very loud voice. (What did he say to them?)

BEVERLY: He said, "People of Mud! Hear what I have to say!"

CARL: And he said, "I will give half my kingdom to anyone who will travel to the Rain God and beg him to stop all this rain."

TEACHER: And Carl, did anyone volunteer to go?

CARL: Yes. *I* volunteered to go!

TEACHER: Because you are called, Carl the Warrior, is that right?

CARL: (Nods his head vigorously).

TEACHER: And since Carl the Warrior was so big and strong and brave, all the people shouted their approval. "Yes, send Carl. We want Carl to go." (And then what?)

DOROTHY: And then Carl quickly gathered up his things and marched to the North.

TEACHER: Yes, but halfway to the Castle of the Rain God the rain turned into snow.

EVELYN: And Carl had only his raincoat and nothing else to keep him warm.

TEACHER: What kind of man was this warrior? Was he a man with ideas as well as muscles?

CARL: (Again nods his head vigorously).

TEACHER: Suddenly the warrior got a wonderful idea for keeping warm. (What was it?)

FRANCES: I know! I know! He dug a hole in the snow and went to sleep.

So on they went, improvising right to the end of the story. On the next day or so Mr. Lubway would bring in copies of the complete and transcribed story for them to read to a partner and to illustrate. This is just a sample of the many approaches he used to involve each student and encourage them to want to read and write. Mr. Lubway knew that if the students were motivated, they would read and write more often and more successfully with each experience. The variety of activities that Lubway used to inspire his students to want to read and write seemed endless. He helped them read plays together and then create their own plays. He had them read and study in order to recreate historical events, multicultural customs, and biographies—

all of this through spontaneous creative drama. His classroom was always dynamic, with students too busy with their discovery and creativity to realize they were learning how to read and write better than ever. (In Part E you'll find more ways of inspiring your students to generate their own intrinsic motivation to read.)

A Teacher Who Provided Effective Extrinsic Motivation for Reading

Frances Hopkins, a teacher I observed on several occasions, also believed in emotions and motivations as the "spark plugs for the learning-to-read-and-write engine." She was bright and bouncy, characteristics that enhanced her playful teaching and her businesslike determination to get every student on the reading path. She was such a highly respected teacher in Jefferson School, her principal continually begged her to take one more of the "unmotivated kids," as he called them.

Like Ray Lubway, Frances Hopkins was determined to lead them eventually to the point of reading for intrinsic reasons. Being a complete realist, though, she first emphasized extrinsic motivation devices, which she referred to as her "bag of tricks." Because most of her students were from families and cultures that emphasized total-family enterprises, her bag of tricks included several ambitious cooperative projects. My favorite community project of hers was the combined "Book Projects" and "Book Shelf Project."

Hopkins's Provision of Extrinsic Motivation through Book Projects and "Bookshelves"

On one wall of her classroom I saw a gigantic vertical thermometer painted on a sheet of butcher paper. Rising from the floor to the ceiling was a thermometer adults use for money drives such as "Help Us Get To The Top: One Million Dollars for Research on Prostate and Breast Cancer." (It has always amazed me how successful those kinds of cooperative races to the finish can be.) In this case Mrs. Hopkins used the vertical thermometer to measure the number of books her entire class had read and recommended to others. The banner she had placed at the top of the thermometer looked like this:

HELP US GET TO THE TOP THIS YEAR WITH 300 BOOKS READ

Frances Hopkins used four procedures for this project:

Step 1: The students are directed to a large illustrated chart on the wall filled with a variety of interesting book projects, most of which the teacher demonstrates (one each day) before they try them. For example:

> Read aloud a very exciting part of your library book to the class. Stop reading right in the middle of the action. Ask three people to guess what happened next. Then tell the class, "You'll have to read the book to find out exactly what happened."
>
> Or, play "Twenty Questions" with the class. Have them think of the object you have in mind that was very important in the book you just read. But first tell them whether the object is "animal, vegetable, or mineral." The game ends after someone guesses correctly or after twenty questions have been asked.
>
> "Twenty Questions" is very useful, not only for interesting students in particular books but also for developing thinking and listening skills. It's also a good game for encouraging every student to contribute and succeed.
>
> Or, plan and present a short skit about a scene in a book that you and a friend read together. Try to use many of the words that the characters said.
>
> Or, write and illustrate a colorful advertisement for the book you have just read. Include the things that would make your classmates want to read the book. Also write where they can find the book, and place your ad in the best place for others to read it, on the bulletin board, the "classroom classified page," or pass it out as a business flyer.
>
> Or, write a letter to a friend and try to get her to read the book you just read. At sharing time you may read to the class part or all of the letter you received in return.

Step 2: For each book a student reads, and does a project on, she receives a "book-back" made from thin colored cardboard or thick colored paper. The color the student receives depends on the genre of the book, e.g., blue for mystery, red for adventure, pink for humorous, and so on. This one-by-six-inch pseudo book-back is written on by the student in the same manner as most actual book-backs, with the title, author, and pretend-publisher, using gold ink or another shiny color can make it even more attractive. The student writes her name on the other side so this project doesn't become a race among individuals but a cooperative race against time. ("Let's go, team, see how many more we can read before the school year comes to a close.")

Step 3: The pseudo book-back is then attached by the student to the pseudo book shelf, which can be made of butcher paper or bulletin board cork, allowing the "shelf" to be prominently displayed in the classroom all year long. The result is an ever-expanding panorama of color across the top of your chalkboard or other area in your classroom. (I have used this idea many times and have found it to be enjoyable and challenging at all grade levels from second through eighth. I've never tried it at lower or higher grades.) Warning: For eager groups of students you'll need a band of butcher paper or cork near the tops of *two* walls!

Both Hopkins and I have discovered the need to give our students at least two twenty-minute periods per week to share their books through book projects. I have also found that those twenty minutes can also be spent as "book selling" experiences: After a student shares his book he then asks "Who would like to read this book next?" The number of raised hands will give the student an idea of how successful his communication and selling techniques were.

Step 4: At the end of the school year the pseudo book-backs are unattached and returned to their owners to take home. Some teachers like to give their students an additional award during the year for each book: A piece of candy per book, or one minute of your time for every five books to play their favorite table game with them. Some teachers even pay them money by the book. However, I have found that using money encourages some students to cheat, *vehemently.* This result defeats your purposes of (1) getting them to actually read more books, (2) encouraging them to read a greater variety of genres, and (3) moving them closer to reading primarily for intrinsic purposes.

Myth 7, Part B: Research That Refutes the Seventh Myth.

To better understand the seventh myth of reading, you and I will need to look more closely at teaching procedures that effectively inspire motivation to read, while also cutting down on stress and anxiety.

1. How do your teaching procedures lead to intrinsic or extrinsic motivation to read, and how do your teaching procedures lead to lack of motivation or even the antimotivation to read?
2. How can teachers cut down on the anxiety and inferiority many students feel?

Whereas the 1980s was the decade of research on reading comprehension strategies, the 1990s might be considered the decade of research on reading motivation. Studies on motivation have been designed to answer a variety of questions, some of which we'll now examine. Please note that each study or research survey will attend to different clusters of the following ten questions:

1. Is reading motivation a single-dimension or multifaceted impulse?
2. What effect does motivation have on reading achievement?
3. What does interest have to do with motivation?
4. What does a student's belief about her reading-competence have to do with her motivation to read?
5. What types of stress or "stressors" influence a student's motivation to read or not to read?
6. How can reading motivation be assessed? (See Part D.)
7. Can nonfiction provide as much pleasure and motivation as fiction?
8. What administrative and parental pressures lead to teacher stress and consequent student anxiety about learning to read well?
9. What role does "choice" have in reading motivation?
10. How can goal setting activate motivation to read?

Studies on the Varied Forms of Motivation to Read

Baker, L. & Wigfield, A. (1999). Dimensions of children's motivation for reading and their relations to reading activity and reading achievement. *Reading Research Quarterly, 34,* 4, 452–477.

Results and Conclusions

1. The variety of reading motivations, confirmed by factor analysis of the *Motivation for Reading Questionnaire,* includes the following:
   a. Self-perception (seeing oneself) as an effective reader;
   b. Enjoying the challenge of reading something difficult;

c. Curiosity about a new and different topic;
d. Involvement in a story plot or identification with a character;
e. Urgent awareness of the importance of learning to read well;
f. Need for recognition by others for skill in reading;
g. Desire for good grades in reading.

2. The ten motivation scales on the *Motivation for Reading Questionnaire* were endorsed by 300 fifth- and sixth-grade students in a highly differential way, with very few students having the same endorsement profiles.

Comment. For example, one student might highly endorse e, f, and g, (the "eager competitor" motivations for reading), while another student might highly endorse b, c, and d (the "book lover" motivation for reading).

3. Students who feel they are good readers—and are intrinsically motivated to read—appear to be the ones who read the most, according to self-reports.
4. Assessment of motivation to read seems to be more accurate with frequency of choosing to read than to students' reading achievement based on standardized scores.
5. No significant relation was found between students' reading motivations and their family income.
6. No significant relation was found between students' reading motivations and their ethnicity.

Comment. Perhaps you are now convinced that the jewel called "reading motivation" has many sparkling facets. Some researchers, though, feel we have ignored the largest facet of all. If you will examine the next review of research, you'll see what I mean.

Urdan, T. C., & Maehr, M. T. (1995). Beyond a two-goal theory of motivation and achievement: A case for social goals. *Review of Educational Research, 65,* 3, 213–243.

Conclusions

1. "Research on academic achievement motivation has...focused on two particular types of achievement goals: task goals and ability goals. A more thorough understanding of motivation and achievement in schools can be developed if we examine social goals...in addition to task and ability goals" (p. 213).

2. One social motivation for academic success is to bring honor to the student's family. Another social motivation for academic success is to maintain friendships with those peers who are also successful. The relationship between social motivation and achievement can be highly complex.

Comment. Highly complex indeed, and highly individual. Let's add to the complexity by inserting another social motivator, namely "family reading attitudes and reading frequency."

Motivation Studies on Interests and Making Choices

Baker, L., Scher, D. and Mackler, K. (1997). Home and family influences on motivations for reading. *Educational Psychologist, 32,* 2, 69–82.

Conclusions

1. Parents who are interested and entertained by their own reading habit tend to hand on that view to their children.
2. Parents who emphasize reading skills rather than enjoyment tend to pass on a less favorable desire to reading.
3. Early childhood encounters with parents who have an attitude of enjoyment and interest toward reading tend to encourage children to read both frequently and broadly.
4. Parents seem to be most attuned to their children's interest or lack of "interest in reading," a concept that is "aligned most closely with intrinsic motivation" (p. 70).

Comment. The conclusions on interest as a motivator tie in directly with conclusions on choice as a motivator.

Morrow, L. M. (1992). The impact of a literature-based program on literacy achievement, use of literature, and attitudes of children from minority backgrounds. *Reading Research Quarterly, 27,* 3, 251–275.

Results and Conclusions

1. Subjects consisting of 72 Black, 62 White, 23 Asian, and 9 Hispanic second graders from 9 classrooms, 2 schools, and 1 school district were motivated by an intense literature-based program to read an average of fifteen books per student between November and April.

2. One of the main motivators, as indicated by interviews, was making choices, such as what to read or write and whether to read or write alone or with others. Those choices and other similar choices motivated literacy activities among advanced, slow, and special-needs children alike.
3. Other high motivators were: (a) being allowed to read "a lot," (b) opportunities to tell felt stories, tape stories, and "chalk talks," (c) the chance to read in a happy social environment.
4. The teachers involved in the study changed their attitudinal stance from (a) fear of taking too much time away from the basal program to (b) wanting literature to become an integral part of their reading program to (c) allowing students to make choices necessarily means allowing them some autonomy.

Comment: When novelty is available for students and teachers, at the very same time, the near-perfect state of motivation has been achieved.

Guthrie, J. T. (1996). Educational contexts for engagement in literacy. *The Reading Teacher, 49,* 6, 432–445.

Conclusions

1. Intense collaboration mixed with autonomy while learning about a topic, problem, or theme has proven to be highly motivating.
2. Abundant research shows that autonomy can lead to intrinsic motivation.
3. When teachers support autonomy by encouraging free expression of opinions, providing choice of learning tasks, and inviting students to participate in decision making, students increase their commitment to learning.

Comment: Is it possible that providing students with the daily period of autonomy (they so desperately need in order to learn) is seen as a threat by many teachers, parents, professors, administrators, and educational publishers? If so, isn't there some way for all concerned to move beyond this insecurity?

A Study of Motivation through Payment of Cash

Now let's look at another form of insecurity (or anxiety), one that causes us to motivate students to read by paying them cold hard cash.

McNinch, G. W. (1997). Earning by learning: Changing attitudes and habits in reading. *Reading Horizons, 37*, 3, 188–194.

Results and Conclusions

1. By paying $2.00 per book to 20 at-risk second and third graders during a half-day six-week summer program, students were able to read "829 books."
2. The top reader completed 56 books and received $112. The least capable (or motivated) reader read 15 books.
3. The total number of 20 children earned (or cost) $1,658.
4. The mean (average) response to a 20-item attitude survey (toward school reading and recreational reading) was 2.8 (neutral) on the pretest; 3.1 (mildly excited) on the posttest. The difference was "statistically significant" (the difference is probably not a chance difference).
5. The mean (average) recreational reading response (10 items) was 3.0 (mildly positive) on the pretest and 3.1 (mildly excited) on the posttest. (Could easily have occurred by chance. No statistically significant difference.)
6. The mean academic reading response (10 items) was 2.8 (neutral) on the pretest and 3.0 (mildly positive) on the posttest. (The difference is not statistically significant.)
7. On the research question, "Will the cash awards result in a positive change in children's school behavior by the end of the first four months of the following school year?" the six teachers were asked if there was a positive change in students' behavior, and the results were these:

Observed Characteristic	% of Teachers Noticing Change
Improved self-esteem	84% of the six teachers
Rise in overall school grades	72% of the six teachers
Rise in reading levels	63% of the six teachers
Improved school attitude	86% of the six teachers

8. Immersing children in a book rich environment staffed by caring volunteers, and rewarding reading with cash incentives seem, at least in the short run, to have created successful readers, even with at-risk children.

Comments on How You Can Design Better Action Research. I'm afraid the $1,658 might have been wasted on an incomplete research plan. I chose this study to provide you with practice in designing much better teacher-involved "action research." Rather than telling you what made the results of this study inaccurate and invalid, I'll ask you to find answers to the following questions by looking again at the previous description of the study.

1. Was there a comparison with a control group that did not get the special summer treatment and the cash?

2. Were the children chosen randomly from a larger population?

3. How were the results biased by using only volunteers as the subjects?

4. Were each of the three motivations controlled in such a way that the cash reward as motivator was separated from the other two motivators, "immersion in a book rich environment" and "a staff of caring volunteers"? In short, which of those three made the real difference?

5. Was the "statistically significant difference" between the pretest and posttest means (averages) the same as the practical difference between those means? How much numerical difference would it take to make the difference between the means a practical consideration for you and your students—5% difference, 10%, 15%, 20%? If they did 3% better on the post- than the pretest, would you consider the summer program a practical one?

6. What is a "statistically significant difference," anyway? And how much was it influenced by the small number of subjects in the study? Would it have been easier to get a statistically significant difference with 100 subjects than with 20 subjects? (The answer: "Definitely!" The more subjects you have the more you rule out chance differences. Chance differences is synonymous with "no significant differences.")

7. Would the pre-post test differences have been the same if the cash award had been left out and the children had been rewarded with "nothing more" than a caring staff and an abundance of good books to read?

8. Might that $1,658 have been better spent on more effective educational motivators? Which ones?

9. Are the differences between the percentages of teachers misleadingly large because there are only six teachers involved? (And were the teachers biased in their responses because of their participation?)

10. And somewhat facetiously, shouldn't that kid who was paid $112 give half of it to his teacher?

The Effects on Motivation of Age, Predeveloped Attitudes, Training in Comprehension Monitoring, and Grades

This raises another question of a more general sort: How durable are the attitudes toward reading as students move through the grades? Do their positive attitudes grow stronger or weaker?

Kush, J. C., & Watkins, M. W. (1996). Long-term stability of children's attitudes toward reading. *Journal of Educational Research, 89,* 5, 315–319.

Results and Conclusions

1. Students who responded in grade 1 and again in grade 4 to McKenna and Kear's *Elementary Reading Attitude Survey* declined in their attitude toward both academic and recreational reading from a mean (average) of 101 to a mean of 97 over the three-year period.
2. The decline was statistically significant and considered to be "somewhat alarming."

Comment. Once again we find the concept of "significant" based on the number of subjects in the study rather than on the practical meaning of the size of the decline. The decline was only 4% over 3 years, a 1.33% drop per year. Alas, like any new activity in life, our enthusiasm for it gradually declines. This was acknowledged by the authors when they stated that the consistent decline was to be expected. Furthermore, they pointed out that the results were consistent with four other declination studies in 1976, 1985, 1991, and 1994.

3. As usual the girls expressed more positive attitudes toward reading than boys, although mostly with recreational rather than academic reading. "This study augments the growing body of evidence regarding young boys' negative reading attitudes" (p. 318).

Comment. A rather uncalled-for remark about boys, don't you think? It's true that there have been nearly three times as many boys as girls placed in learning disability programs. It is not true that boys automatically have negative attitudes toward reading (although they might have negative attitudes toward others or themselves). In this very study, the difference between fourth-grade boys and girls on attitudes toward academic reading was 25.07 to 25.48, a difference of only 0.41, which is 1.6%.

It would take too much of your time for me to go into this age-old issue. Suffice it to say that the problem is not just boys with a "negative attitude," but overworked teachers who haven't been given enough time and training to adjust both to gender differences in learning to read and to learning differences within each gender and culture. Let's just move on, shall we?

Payne, B. D. & Manning, B. H. (1992). Basal reading instruction: Effects of comprehension monitoring training on reading comprehension, strategy use and attitude. *Reading research and instruction, 32,* 1, 29–38.

Conclusion. "Average fourth grade readers who received metacognitive skills training had greater reading comprehension, greater knowledge about reading strategies, and *more positive attitudes toward reading* than children in the control group."

Comment. On the one hand, we can't generalize the results, because the subjects consisted of only 20 students from the experimental classroom and 11 control students from another classroom. They represented only themselves and not a larger population. I suppose it's too bad they weren't all given a number placed on a ping pong ball. Then the balls could have been shaken up in a large container and distributed evenly into two clusters, the experimental students and the control students. This simple procedure might have given the experiment a little less bias and a little more validity.

On the other hand, this piece of action research gives us a hint that possibly the teaching of comprehension self-monitoring can lead to greater success in reading, and therefore a greater sense of self-effectiveness as a reader. Let's look at more studies of this important motivator—the self-effectiveness that good readers feel. Researchers refer to those feelings either as "competence beliefs, self-confidence, conceptual change, self-efficacy, or its synonym, self-effectiveness."

Bandura, A. (1989). Recognition of cognitive processes through perceived self-efficacy. *Developmental Psychology, 25,* 5, 729–735.

Conclusions

1. "People who believe strongly in their problem-solving capabilities remain highly efficient in their analytic thinking in complex decision-making situations," e.g., deciding on the author's message (p. 729).
2. "Those who are plagued by self-doubts are erratic in their analytic thinking. Quality of analytic thinking, in turn, determines the level of performance accomplishments" (p. 729).
3. "Those who have a high sense of efficacy visualize success scenarios that provide positive guides for performance" (p. 729) (This is very likely behavior, one that all of us experience when we're relaxed or "in the groove" or "in the flow." The possibility of visualization guiding our performance also seems reasonable, don't you think? After all, it's supposed to be the way wolves, lions, and other animals prepare themselves for action. Let's now look at other ways that self-confidence, along with self-relevance, may influence reading motivation and success.)

Wigfield, A., Eccles, J., Yoon, K. W., Harold, R. D., Arbreton, A. J. A., Freedman-Doan, C., & Blumenfeld, P. C. (1997). Change in children's competence beliefs and subjective task values across the elementary school years: A 3-year study. *Journal of Educational Psychology, 89,* 3, 451–469.

Conclusions

1. The ratings of students' reading competence—based on their parents,' their teachers' and their own self-perceptions—were increasingly alike over the three-year period. (Who's influencing whom?)
2. Students' beliefs in their own competence, as well as their notions of the value (relevance) of the reading task, have a major impact on their motivation and success.
3. Their prior performances as a reader, as well as the feedback provided by adults, also have a major impact on their motivation and success.
4. "Both mothers' and teachers' ratings of children's competence relate more strongly to children's own competence beliefs than they do to children's interest in the different activities" (p. 462).

Comment. I have no idea what #4 means. Do you? Clarity of research reports is the single most wanted item in educational and other social sciences.

What about grades? Aren't they part of a student's feelings of reading competence?

Thomas, S. & Oldfather, P. (1997). Intrinsic motivations, literacy, and assessment practices: "That's my grade. That's me." *Educational Psychologist, 32*, 2, 107–123.

Conclusions

1. Assessment practices, especially grades, affect students' motivations to read, in both a positive and a negative way.
2. Grades can have the effect of reducing the self-determination of the learner.

Comment. The reduction of students' self-determination that I have witnessed includes: (a) having to ignore their own special individual way of learning, (b) being required to read for the purpose of answering the *teacher's* questions rather than reading for personal relevance, (c) not being asked to determine what is important and relevant to them. Instead they read for the grade and then forget about it.

3. "Students perceived that grades shifted their goal orientations away from learning or mastery goals, toward concern with ego or performance goals..." (p. 118).
4. Secondary school students felt that the emphasis on grades rather than on specific feedback made it difficult to improve their knowledge and skills.
5. "Although many saw themselves as 'selling out' for grades in high school, they felt that their early experiences in elementary school...had some impact in supporting their continuing impulse to learn" (p. 118).

How Do Emotional Stress, Anxiety, and Depression Affect Students' Reading Difficulties?

Werner, P. H. (1985). *The symptoms of childhood depression as factors in children's reading difficulties.* Unpublished dissertation. North Texas State University, 241 pages.

Results

1. Almost 45% (30) of the 67 children who were referred to the Pupil Appraisal Center For Reading Difficulties at North Texas State University showed clear symptoms of depression.
2. Out of 29 types of depression symptoms—categorized into the four clusters of emotional, social, physiological, and educational—emotional symptoms were observed the most. The two most noticeable symptoms were feelings of anxiety and inadequacy.
3. The instructional reading levels of most of the children were at or above grade level. (So why were they sent to the Pupil Appraisal Center For *Reading* Difficulties? Give it some thought.)
4. After evaluation by PAC staff, 67% were referred for both counseling and "remedial" reading instruction; 20% were referred for counseling only; 10% were referred for "remedial" reading instruction only.

Comment. This is a clear illustration of how much a student's emotional condition can influence his or her ability to learn to read well. It is also an illustration of how often we teachers may blame reading problems instead of emotional problems for ineffective reading.

Breznitz, Z. (1991). Anxiety and reading comprehension: A longitudinal study of Israeli pupils. *Reading Improvement, 20,* 0, 89–95.

Results and Conclusions

1. Students with a low sociometric score (low peer esteem) and a high anxiety score correspondingly scored poorly on oral and silent reading comprehension.
2. Those students showing high anxiety and low peer esteem scored lower on oral reading comprehension than silent reading comprehension.

Comment. See Part E for ideas on how to counteract these problems.

Gentile, L. M., & McMillan, M. M. (1987). *Stress and reading difficulties: Research, assessment, intervention.* Newark, DE: International Reading Association.

Conclusions

1. Teaching procedures that cause the most anxiety and stress for poor readers are reading out loud publicly and being required to read materials that are too difficult for them.

2. Another major cause is that of providing monotonous assignments similar to worksheets.
3. An even more damaging practice is to totally focus on a student's weaknesses rather than providing positive reinforcement.

How Can Learning and Reading Become More Enjoyable and Motivating?

I have saved this research question for last, because enjoyment seems to be so fundamental to motivation. In the long run we're all searching for joy, even those who are motivated to get out of their present danger or misery.

I came across this next and last research report through the help of my colleague, Louise Fulton. For forty years Dr. Fulton has been involved in teaching and motivating students of a great variety: "normal" elementary and high school students, children who are deaf and blind, children with learning disabilities or behavior disorders, and university students of numerous ethnic groups. Dr. Fulton was kind enough to provide me with her brief summary of a research report by a famous psychologist at the University of Chicago, Mihali Csikszentmihali (Cheek-sent-me-high-ee). Dr. Csikszentmihali is the author of several books on education and human development and has spent over thirty years studying the phenomenon called "enjoyment," the source of motivation. Please note the depth of his research methodology and his insights into the causes of motivation and enjoyment.

Csikszentmihali, M. (1998). *Finding flow: The psychology of engagement with everyday life.* New York: Basic Books.

Procedures. At first he interviewed people, directly, face to face, from all over the world, tapping their memories of various experiences and how they felt when they were having the experience. This provided him with many ideas about enjoyment but the information was much too general. Consequently, he devised a research method that he called ESP, Experience Sampling Method. This method allowed him to obtain information from people at the very moment of their experiences.

Each of his research subjects was equipped with a beeper and a notebook filled with blank response sheets. From 8 to 10 times a day, for a full week, he contacted each of his subjects to ask them the standard questions, such as "Where are you now?" "What are you doing?" "Who is with you?" "Specifically, how are you feeling about yourself," and so on.

Conclusions. There are eight key factors that make up enjoyment (which he refers to as "flow." (Note how similar these eight factors are to those factors of motivation other researchers have discovered.) Csikszentmihali's eight factors include: (1) a clear goal, (2) feedback, (3) challenges that match skills, (4) concentration, (5) focus, (6) control, (7) loss of self-consciousness, and (8) transformation of time.

Comments from Dr. Fulton

A clear goal. Why do students get more involved in a game than in reading? Could it be that they fully understand the procedures involved in the game and know what they must do to win? Do we as teachers provide students with the procedures involved in the game of reading and how to win that game?

Feedback. Why do some students spend so much of their time looking around to see what their peers are doing? Could it be that we as teachers are not arranging for all students (secure and insecure) to receive that vital input from others—that pat on the back that keeps them motivated?

Challenge matching skills. Are we as teachers using our observation skills to notice whether each student is bored or frustrated or moving full-steam-ahead?

Concentration. Do we provide a learning environment that permits each student to truly concentrate, or do we allow their motivation to be dissipated by noise, hostility, embarrassment, or lack of learning tools?

Focus. How often do our students become so focused on learning or reading that they forget everything else?

Control. Do our students feel that they are in control of their life in the classroom? Do they get to make enough choices on their own about books, about writing in their journals, about projects they really want to participate in?

Loss of self-consciousness. Do our students feel safe from ridicule—so safe that they can be interested in reading and learning? So they don't have to put so much energy into "being cool"?

Transformation of time. Does time fly for our students or are they so uninvolved in their learning and reading that the hands on the clock seem to be stuck? Perhaps the best assessment of learning is that remark we long to hear: "Gosh, is the class over already?"

Myth 7, Part C: A Case Study Showing the Effects on a Teacher Who Believes the seventh myth.

The teacher I have chosen as my case study is myself. Why? Because no one has made more mistakes than I have!!

A Teacher Who Provided Antieffective Motivation for Reading

My first year of teaching young learners was one I engaged in mostly for the opportunity to save up enough money to finish my studies the following year at Antioch College. The Mad River School District near Dayton, Ohio was desperate for a male teacher to teach boys physical education half the day and a sixth-grade classroom the other half. Being poor and very naive I took the job without any training. I did all right with the physical education classes, but with the sixth-grade class I bombed an average of twice a minute for the first three months.

Allow me to describe for you a few of my mistakes in attempting to provide those sixth graders with motivation to read. (To tell you about all the other mistakes would be too cruel to myself.) Every day during the first three months I would motivate them to read in this manner:

> Group One, read the story starting on page 79 of the blue book; Group Two, read the story starting on page 48 of the red book; Group Three, the story starting on page 31 of the yellow book.

> I might as well have been a church leader commanding his flock to sing three different hymns at the same time. It doesn't take much teaching talent to motivate students by calling out the page.

While my students labored away without any prereading vocabulary or schema enhancement, I methodically copied three sets of questions on the board that I dutifully read from the three different Teacher Guides. (Again, no teaching going on. Merely testing them on their cognitive "comprehension.") I felt very proud of myself, simply because I was now a teacher—and getting paid for it too. So, in essence, I was highly motivated and they were antimotivated, a state of being I was to observe several years later, during at least half of my numberless observations of teachers, student teachers, and their students.

Did we sit down together and discuss the emotional aspects of the literature they had read? *Of course not.* Did we share our interpretations, our opinions, our feelings, our ideas for exploring further information or stories by the author? *Nonsense.* Did we turn the stories into narration and dialogue so we could interpret them in dramatic format? *Never.* It was far more motivating for me to keep those restless noisy preteenagers quietly scribbling answers at their thirty-five individual desks. (From the looks on their faces, though, I'd have to say they were now doubly antimotivated.)

Some Other Ways I Generated Antieffective Motivation for Reading

In time my students grew rebellious, of course. And this meant that I had to "motivate" them by "disciplining" them. (At that time the word *discipline* referred to punishment rather than its original meaning of "developing the precision of your mind.") And how did I now motivate them? Did I teach them more about the discipline called "reading" by modeling a few comprehension strategies (in an interesting way)?

Did I humorously model how I monitor my own comprehension? Uhh-uhh. That might have been too cognitive for them (and even more so for me). Instead, I used every single punishment I had observed or experienced during my own schooling. Here's a very abbreviated list of them, in case you're inclined to believe that teachers should be hired to discipline the troops rather than inspire them.

Require them to write 200 times. "I will always read my book quietly without disturbing the reading time of my teacher and his other students." I fooled myself into thinking that this form of motivation worked very well, although I was appalled by their illegible handwriting. For some reason their sentences didn't flow like real sentences. They looked more like piles of different train cars, with all 200 of the "always" cars piled up in one wobbly column and all 200 of the "read" cars piled up in a nearby wobblier column. Naturally the "quietly" cars were so frightened they became impossible to read.

I will always read my book quietly.
I will always read my book quietly.
I will always read my book quietly.
I will always read my book quietly.
I will always read my book quietly.
I will always read my book quietly.
I will always read my book quietly
I will always read my book quietly
I will always read my book quietly
I will always read my book quietly.
I will always read my book quietly.
I will always read my book quietly.

Demand their attention by slapping my ruler down on my desk. (This worked pretty well, until I broke my ruler right in front of them.)

Make them stand in the corner if they weren't really reading. (This worked for a day or two, but suddenly all of the boys were highly "motivated" to take their turn in the corner. Often we ran out of corners.)

Early in the fourth month I had coffee with one of the other sixth-grade teachers and asked her for suggestions on how to "get my kids to read." She was very helpful and said, "I reward them for reading rather than punishing them." That made a lot of sense to me, so I started rewarding them the very next day. For every five-minute period the whole class read without stopping, I passed out two dollars of monopoly money to each and every one of them. (I owned two sets of Monopoly.)

This worked for only the first five minutes, and then it fell apart. They rebelled about the pay scale and demanded real money instead. We had a nice little discussion about the matter, during which time I realized I was finally "relating" to my students. After much fruitful and unfruitful negotiation we agreed that I was just a poor teacher and I could only afford a dime apiece for each of two twenty-minute blocks of solid reading. (The dime back then is equivalent to 60 cents today.)

Well, as I said to you earlier, it doesn't pay to pay. By the end of the week I was out of dimes—and out $35 on my grocery budget. Not only that, I felt certain that most of the boys were just staring at the same page for the whole twenty-minute period. Just think of the fantasies they must have been creating with their fertile greedy minds during all that time.

To draw this depiction to a close, I'd like to report to you that it took me the full year to gradually learn these things:

1. I really had to inspire rather than hire.
2. What they wanted to learn through reading was far more important than what I wanted them to learn about reading.
3. Writing independently about their own problems and interests led to much more real reading (sharing among peers) than lackadaisical reading about book characters' problems and interests.
4. Attempting to solve real problems (like the lack of traffic guides and stoplights near the school) led to much more reading (newspapers, letters, state laws) and writing (letters to authorities, legislators, and neighbors) than most of them had ever done in their lives.
5. Paying attention to students' feelings about reading and writing can be more important, at times, than paying such strict attention to canned reading assignments plucked out of teacher guides and those too specific district and state manuals.
6. Kids of any age from 1 to 99 enjoy being read to. No better reading motivator.

> My students, ever since the beginning of my first year, have been my main teachers, especially when it comes to learning and motivation.

What My Students (and My Research Colleagues) Have Taught Me about Motivation Principles

Most students of mine have eventually become motivated learners, but only when I have consistently behaved toward them in these ways:

1. When I have given my first attention to their basic human needs for a sense of belonging and self-esteem in both the classroom and school community. This has meant taking the time in our community life to:

   a. Celebrate each student's progress and special talents in learning to read, write, think, and live well.
   b. Communicate at least 90% of the time with warm, constructive, positive words and gestures. (I'm too human to hit 100%).
   c. Try to make each one of them actually feel my genuine affection, respect, and concern for them.
   d. Notice their positive characteristics more than their immature characteristics.
   e. Make the importance of each student well known to the rest of the classroom community.

2. When I have consistently tried to teach my students at the appropriate level of difficulty (or in Vygotsky's words, "at their zone of proximal development"). This has meant taking time in our classroom community to:
   a. Check students' readiness for the next step by listening to them read aloud or contribute during discussions, and by noticing their frustration or boredom.
   b. Provide extra instruction to those who miscue with false substitutes and no-shows.
   c. Help struggling readers find interesting library books at their level of difficulty.
   d. Move students individually and gradually up the cognition scale of Bloom's Taxonomy from knowledge to comprehension to application to analysis synthesis to evaluation, fully expecting my students to differ from each other in their levels of thinking and responding.

3. When I have consistently found ways to provide frequent and specific individual feedback. This has meant taking time in our classroom community to:
   a. Respond specifically and promptly to comments in students' journals, staying in the student's mode of thinking and feeling and providing the student with a response that's interesting to read.
   b. Praise specifically and immediately during discussions or book sharing, rather than relying only on "good job" and other trite forms of approval.
   c. Mentor briefly while the student is writing, not only after the composition has been completed to the student's satisfaction.

- **d.** Provide enough easy but interesting text so that feedback is intrinsically provided by the student's own successful predictions and confirmations.
- **e.** Have students work as feedback partners during "repeated reading" activities. (But first teach all of them how to provide positive feedback.)
- **f.** Provide students with feedback that helps them feel good about their own success rather than their ability to please the teacher.

4. When I have consistently found ways to provide novelty in my presentation of ideas and in my adaptations of learning activities. This has meant taking time in our classroom community to:

- **a.** Share reading experiences in different parts of the classroom.
- **b.** Gradually vary the book sharing from groups of two to groups of three, four, and more.
- **c.** Vary my reading aloud to students, e.g., using a prop or wearing an item of clothing that fits the clothing or manner of the main character in the book.
- **d.** Learn new words through games, dialogue, and miming.
- **e.** Read varied genres aloud to my students.
- **f.** Let each student have a chance to lead a book discussion, literature circle, or book club.
- **g.** Provide the classroom with a varied library from which to choose their own books. Allow as much time for reading chosen books as for reading required books.

To remember those four motivation principles think of this statement:

NOVELTY NEEDS LEVEL FEEDBACK

Add novelty to your students' learning experiences.

Take care of students' basic needs for security, belonging, and self-esteem.

Teach at the appropriate level of difficulty.

Provide frequent and specific feedback.

In Part D you will find ideas on assessing the various motivations of your students "to read or not to read," isn't that the question?

Myth 7, Part D: Ideas for Assessing Students' and Teachers' Beliefs about the Seventh Myth.

Self-Check for the Teacher ______________________
Date ________

______ **1.** At the beginning of the school year I individually interview my students to determine what they think reading is, what they like to read, why they like to read, and what help they would like from me.

______ **2.** I create a print-rich environment in the classroom to help my students remember and appreciate what they have learned.

______ **3.** I like to tease my students' curiosity about books by reading parts of them or acting out a scene from the book (with the help of a good reader).

______ **4.** I have my students learn a great deal about one topic so they can feel that reading can make them an expert.

______ **5.** I try to have each parent for each child observe our literacy program in the classroom at least once during the first half of the school year. I'm very willing to tie in a parent–teacher conference on the same day they observe.

______ **6.** I send letters to parents with ideas on how to motivate more reading at home.

______ **7.** I make sure that reading is enjoyable by motivating my students to read more books by a particular author we have already read aloud and whose life we have learned about.

______ **8.** I use intriguing topics in science and social studies to motivate different small groups of students to read.

______ **9.** I usually discuss with my students the relevance of a book, topic, or current event to their own lives and ambitions.

______ **10.** I use varied means of letting students share what they are reading with peers.

______ **11.** I read aloud to my students (of any age) using a different genre each time. At the same time, I assess the variety of genres each of them is reading.

______ **12.** I quite often rely on reading games to help them enjoy their practice sessions on recognizing words.

______ **13.** Whenever I can, I bring in older students to read with my students.

______ **14.** Student publishing of their own books happens in my classroom very often.

______ **15.** I have my students read books out loud in front of other students only when they are enthusiastic about this privilege.

______ **16.** I seldom interrupt my students when they're reading orally or silently. But after they have finished I collaboratively discuss with them the phonic and contextual miscues that changed the author's meaning.

______ **17.** My goal is to have my students stay reasonably relaxed about reading and not anxious or frustrated.

______ **18.** My students are constantly encouraged to choose a book they really want to read.

______ **19.** I allow time for both individual and shared reading.

______ **20.** I seldom push students to read under time pressure.

______ **21.** I do not allow my students to ridicule each other's reading either verbally or with body language.

______ **22.** I treat reading lessons as time for learning together, not as time to "complete the story." They can complete it by themselves later.

______ **23.** With each student I emphasize strengths more than weaknesses.

______ **24.** Although I let children choose most of the books they read, I also keep looking for books that would interest individual students.

______ **25.** I often "reform" a troublemaker by spending more time helping him read well and feel good about his reading ability.

Elementary Reading Attitude Survey

This assessment device was developed by Michael C. McKenna and Dennis J. Kear. It can be administered to the entire class in only ten minutes, as there are only twenty questions for the teacher to read. The students respond by selecting the "Garfield the Cat" pose that matches their feelings—ranging from very positive to very negative. Here are a few examples of questions to read to the students.

> How do you feel when you read a book in school during your free time?
>
> How do you feel about reading instead of playing?
>
> How do you feel about starting a new book?
>
> How do you feel about doing reading workbook pages and worksheets?

Simple administration, scoring, and interpretation procedures, along with the entire twenty questions are available to you in the May 1990 issue of *The Reading Teacher*, pages 626–639. This journal is available in any university library. Because the authors of this survey have placed it in the public domain, you may copy it without getting permission.

Advice. It can be difficult to get a high level of validity or reliability on this "feeling" type of assessment, especially for every group of students that uses it. Normative data were gathered for this survey, but norm scales are only as good as the instrument is valid and reliable. So, why not use it as one estimate of each student's attitude toward reading? Combine it with observations, interviews, and reading workshop experiences in the classroom.

Motivation to Read Profile

This assessment device was developed by Linda B. Gambrell, Barbara Martin Palmer, Rose Marie Codling, and Susan Anders Mazzoni. It consists of two parts, one for group response and one for individual interview response. The Reading Survey has twenty items with a multiple-choice format. It assesses both "self-concept as a reader" and "value of reading." It takes fifteen to twenty minutes to administer. Here are two examples of questions to read to the students.

I read not as well as my friends.
about the same as my friends.
a little better than my friends.
a lot better than my friends.

I tell my friends about good books I read.
I never do this.
I almost never do this.
I do this some of the time.
I do this a lot.

The Conversational Interview. This part of the Motivation to Read Profile has conversational items like these:

Tell me about the most interesting story or book you have read this week.
How did you know or find out about this story?
Why was this story interesting to you?
Tell me about your favorite author.
What do you think you have to learn to be a better reader?

Advice. This is also a self-report instrument, and has the same limitations as the ERAS discussed prior to this one. Like the ERAS, the MRP can not tell you whether the students are responding to please you or to be "correct" about themselves. Therefore, once again, use this as only one form of information. The important thing with each of the surveys is that you can get a glimpse of student's self-perception, which after all is what motivates people anyway.

The MRP has also been placed in the public domain, so you can copy it without getting permission. You'll find the complete survey and directions in the April 1996 issue of *The Reading Teacher,* pages 518–533.

Myth 7, Part E: Suggested Interventions with Students Who Lack in Motivation to Read.

A Summary and Checklist of Motivation Ideas from This Chapter

______ Kids who seem to "survive and thrive" the best during the process of developing literacy are those who believe in themselves. Teachers can influence that major conviction.

______ Intrinsic motivation is a private matter, something secret inside us. Something that says, "Yes, what I'm doing right now is what I desire to do." For maximum motivation, teachers can discover what each child wants to experience and learn and help it happen.

______ Ray Lubway is not the only one who can use spontaneous improvised "drama" and "story creation" for inspiring intrinsic motivation to read, write, listen, and speak. You can do it, too. For best results do this with small and large group projects, keep a relaxed nonjudgmental environment, and avoid putting individuals in the spotlight unless they desire it. (I've always had to remind myself that our goal is literacy development rather than the training of professional writers and actors.)

______ Creative story production and either spontaneous or scripted drama can be used also as exciting literacy motivators "across the curriculum" in mathematics, social studies, music, science, and art.

______ Use Frances Hopkins's method of motivating your students through book projects and "book shelves," and her concept of a "cooperative race to the finish line." A thermometer can also be used to record the cooperative race.

______ Help each student develop a positive self-perception as "a reader who is learning to read even better." Use interesting easy books that allow you to praise the student for a series of small step successes. Ask him to tell you how he read better today. Don't keep him reading at the frustration level. He'll only hate himself or the teacher or schooling in general.

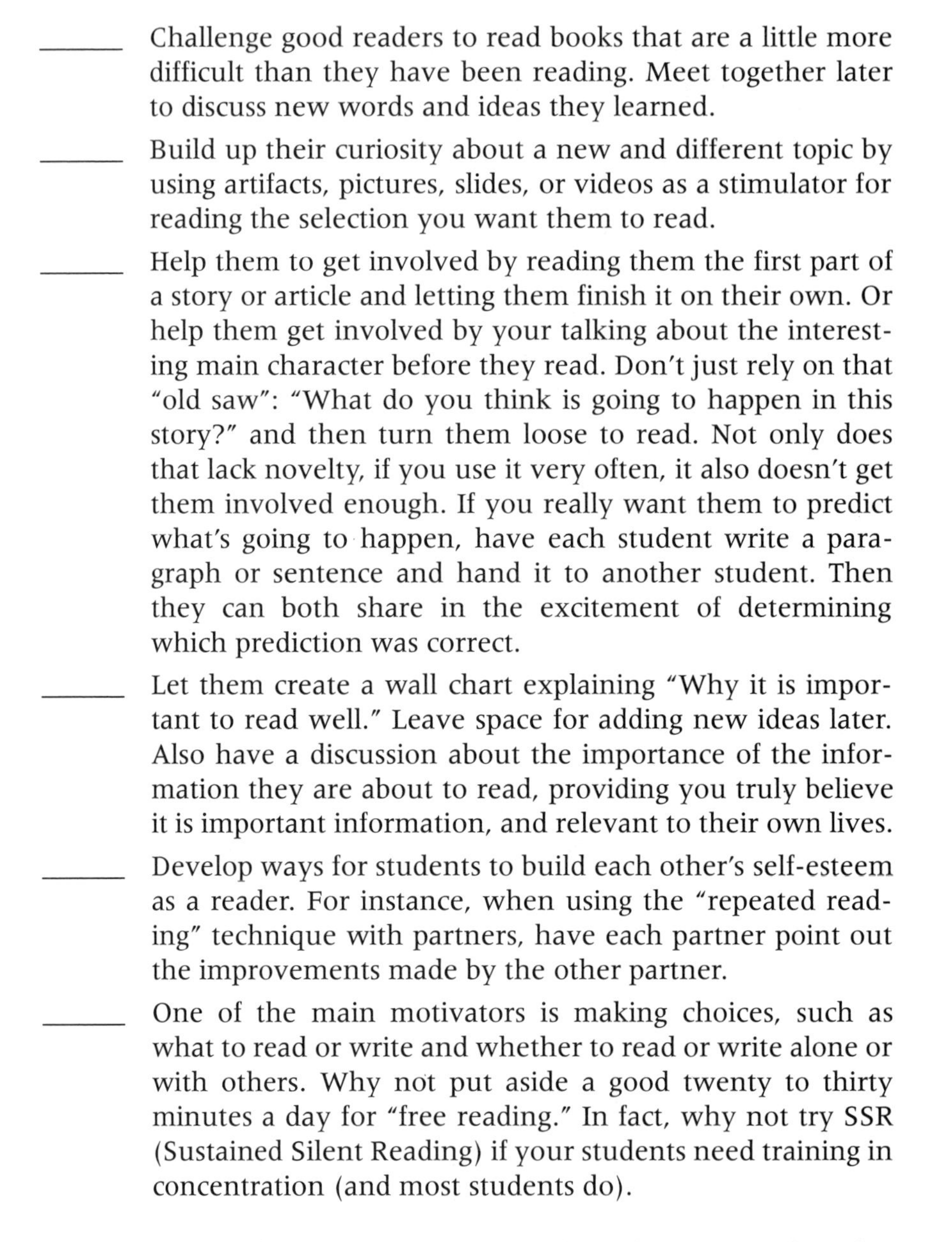

______ Challenge good readers to read books that are a little more difficult than they have been reading. Meet together later to discuss new words and ideas they learned.

______ Build up their curiosity about a new and different topic by using artifacts, pictures, slides, or videos as a stimulator for reading the selection you want them to read.

______ Help them to get involved by reading them the first part of a story or article and letting them finish it on their own. Or help them get involved by your talking about the interesting main character before they read. Don't just rely on that "old saw": "What do you think is going to happen in this story?" and then turn them loose to read. Not only does that lack novelty, if you use it very often, it also doesn't get them involved enough. If you really want them to predict what's going to happen, have each student write a paragraph or sentence and hand it to another student. Then they can both share in the excitement of determining which prediction was correct.

______ Let them create a wall chart explaining "Why it is important to read well." Leave space for adding new ideas later. Also have a discussion about the importance of the information they are about to read, providing you truly believe it is important information, and relevant to their own lives.

______ Develop ways for students to build each other's self-esteem as a reader. For instance, when using the "repeated reading" technique with partners, have each partner point out the improvements made by the other partner.

______ One of the main motivators is making choices, such as what to read or write and whether to read or write alone or with others. Why not put aside a good twenty to thirty minutes a day for "free reading." In fact, why not try SSR (Sustained Silent Reading) if your students need training in concentration (and most students do).

Research and personal experience has shown me that this method, and this form of motivation, work even with first graders, as long as all of these conditions are met:

1. Teachers (and other adults in the room) read too (as models).
2. Each student has access to a variety of books in the room.

3. Wordless picture books are available for the very young.
4. Books read to them at home can be brought to school.
5. Very easy books are available for deficient or inexperienced readers.
6. The timer is set for about three minutes at first, and increased very gradually to twenty minutes or more. (I would increase the time no more than one-half minute per day or two minutes per week. It's less painful for the inexperienced or deficient readers that way.) You may also wish to use the thermometer chart as a cooperative motivator, discussed in relation to Frances Hopkins's book-shelf project. Set your pseudo-thermometer from 3 to 30 "degrees" Centigrade to stand for minutes of SSR (Sustained Silent Reading).
7. Before the timer is set, everyone has been helped to find a book at an appropriate level of difficulty.
8. The SSR program is continued all year long and not dropped after a month or two.

For research on SSR see Kaisen, J. (1987). *The Reading Teacher, 40,* 532–536.

And now, our final motivator will be letter grades. If letter grades are required by parents and administrators in your school district, try developing written criteria for each different grade, spelling out what an "A" and other grades in reading mean in very specific action terms. For instance, "A means that the student (1) reads for the purpose of understanding what an author is saying, (2) skillfully uses phonics, sight words, and the author's meaning to predict and recognize each word in a sentence, (3) frequently chooses to read library books, magazines, and newspapers at home and school, (4) frequently uses a computer as a word processor for both writing and reading."

My Final Suggestion and Request for Your Teaching and Motivating of the Reading/Writing Processes

Please! I beg of you! Help the cause of education by NOT using this criterion for grading: "Completes all his worksheets and workbook pages on time." If you haven't done so already, please give considerable thought to drastically reducing worksheets and workbooks, either as motivators or as teaching tools. A room library of both easy and challenging books is a much better source than worksheets for improving their reading. Let me provide you with some major research support for my request.

Richard Anderson and his colleagues were asked by the U.S. Department of Education to study the U.S. schools and make recommendations on improving reading instruction. This was a Herculean effort involving tens of thousands of students and teachers. Here are some of their findings.

1. Up to 70% of the time set aside for reading instruction was spent on worksheets or workbook pages—explaining how to do them, letting children complete them with little or no supervision, checking them together, or having the teacher check them and hand them back for children to see how many they got right or wrong.

2. It was not unusual for a child to complete one thousand reading worksheets and workbook pages in only one year's time!

3. The use of worksheets and workbooks did not lead to improvement in reading ability. (It merely stole time away from real reading of real books.)

4. The more that complete stories, books, and articles were read by the children, the more their reading ability improved!

5. The average time per day for fifth graders was less than *four* minutes of reading at home, and an average of *130* minutes of watching TV. (Thus, you can see the need for more real reading at school as well as the need for real educating of parents on reading books at home.)

(For the research report, see Anderson, R. C. et al. (1985). *Becoming a nation of readers: The report of the Commission on Reading.* Urbana, IL: Center for the Study of Reading.)

And now we've unclothed those seven tempting myths of reading and found nothing but hot air inside each and every one. My very best wishes to all of you in your efforts to inspire literacy to grow, to extend its enormous benefits toward the happiness and well-being of people all over the world.

APPENDIX A

Fry Word List*

the	of	and	a	to	in	1-6
is	you	that	it	he	was	7–12
for	on	are	as	with	his	13–18
they	I	at	be	this	have	19–24
from	or	one	had	by	words	25–30
but	not	what	all	were	we	31–36
when	you	can	said	there	use	37–42
an	each	which	she	do	how	43–48
their	if	will	up	other	about	49–54
out	many	then	them	these	so	55–60
some	her	would	make	like	him	61–66
into	time	has	look	two	more	67–72
write	go	see	number	no	way	73–78
could	people	my	than	first	water	79–84
been	called	who	oil	its	now	85–90
find	long	down	day	did	get	91–96
come	made	may	part	over	new	97–102
sound	take	only	little	work	know	103–108
place	years	live	me	back	give	109–114
most	very	after	things	our	just	115–120
name	good	sentence	man	think	say	121–126
great	where	help	through	much	before	127–132
line	right	too	means	old	any	133–138
same	tell	boy	following	came	want	139–144
show	also	around	form	three	small	145–150
set	put	end	does	another	well	151–156
large	must	big	even	such	because	157–162
turned	here	why	asked	went	men	163–168
read	need	land	different	home	us	169–174
move	try	kind	hand	picture	again	175–180
change	off	play	spell	air	away	181–186
animals	house	point	page	letters	mother	187–192
answer	found	study	still	learn	should	193–198
American	world	high	every	near	add	199–204
food	between	own	below	country	plants	205–210
last	school	father	keep	trees	never	211–216
started	city	early	eyes	light	thought	217–222
head	under	story	saw	left	don't	223–228
few	while	along	might	close	something	229–234
seemed	next	hard	open	example	beginning	235–240

*From *The Reading Teacher's Book of Lists,* Third Ed., by Edward B. Fry, et al., 1993.

APPENDIX B

Three Phonics Tests

Phonics Test One: The BAF Test

The BAF Test uses nonsense words and is not suitable for children who have not yet succeeded at the primer level or above. It consists of two parts and must be administered individually. Normally this test would be given to children above grade 1 who are considered "remedial readers." You have permission to enlarge and reproduce it.

Part I: Consonant Letters, Digraphs, and Clusters

The children should be encouraged to try decoding each nonsense word without your help. If they miss one, simply circle it and have them continue. Be sure to pronounce the first one for them /baf/ and have them pronounce it correctly before they continue. It is also a good idea to correct the second one if they miss it (caf is pronounced /kaf/). Consider a word wrong only if the target letter, digraph, or blend is wrong. For example, for 1c in Part 1, daf is correct. So is dap, but not paf, since the target letter is d.

Name of Student

Directions to be read or told to the student:

"These words are nonsense words. They are not real words. I'd like you to think about what sounds the letters stand for; then read each word out loud without my help. Don't try to go fast; read the list slowly. If you have any trouble with a word, I'll just circle it and you can go on to the next one. The first word is /baf/. Now you say it....All right, now go on to the rest of the words in row 1."

Consonant Letters

	A	*B*	*C*	*D*	*E*	*F*	*G*
1.	baf	caf	daf	faf	gaf	haf	jaf
2.	kaf	laf	maf	naf	paf	raf	saf
3.	taf	vaf	waf	yaf	zaf	baf	bax

Consonant Digraphs

	A	*B*	*C*	*D*	*E*	*F*	*G*	*H*
4.	chaf	phaf	shaf	thaf	whaf	fack	fang	fank

Consonant Clusters

	A	*B*	*C*	*D*	*E*	*F*	*G*	*H*
5.	blaf	braf	claf	craf	draf	dwaf	flaf	fraf
6.	glaf	graf	fand	plaf	praf	quaf	scaf	scraf
7.	skaf	slaf	smaf	snaf	spaf	splaf	spraf	squaf
8.	staf	straf	swaf	thraf	traf	twaf		

Part II: Vowel Letters, Vowel Digraphs, and Vowel Clusters (For those whose instructional Level is at least Primer)

This part of the inventory should also be administered individually. You will need to enlarge and reproduce a copy of this test for each child. The children should be encouraged to try decoding each nonsense word without your help. If they miss one, simply circle it and have them continue. Be sure to pronounce the first one for them /baf/ and have them pronounce it correctly before they continue.

Directions to be read or told to the student. "These words are nonsense words. They are not real words. I'd like you to think about what sounds the letters stand for; then read each word out loud without any help. Don't try to go fast; read the list slowly. If you have any trouble with a word, I'll circle it and you can go on to the next one. The first word is /baf/. Now you say it.... All right, now go on to the rest of the words in row 1."

	A	*B*	*C*	*D*	*E*	*F*	*G*
1.	baf	bafe	barp	baif	bawf		
2.	bef	befe	berf	beaf			
3.	bof	bofe	borf	boaf	bouf	boif	boof
4.	bif	bife	birf				
5.	buf	bufe	burf				

Phonics Test Two: The Phonogram Phonics Test

This test will give you an idea of how well a student can recognize patterns of letters at the end of one-syllable words or at the end of syllables in multisyllabic words.

High-Frequency Phonogram Test

Name of Student ________________ Grade __________

zab	zack	zace	zail	zay	zall	zed	zell	zeak
zear	zid	zick	zice	zight	zob	zock	zoke	zold
zout	zom	zore	zub	zuck	zy	zad	zamp	zade
zain	zar	zen	zeal	zew	zend	zig	zill	zide
zag	zand	zake	zark	zaw	zam	zame	zang	zash
zan	zank	zet	zim	zent	zeam	zing	zime	zod
zong	zone	zud	zump	zunt	zap	zate	zest	zat
zane	zug	zeat	zin	zish	zint	zeep	zatch	zeed
zog	zum	zip	zink	zone	zope	zun	zut	zive
zot	zuff	zunk	zeet	zung	zow	zown	zab	zack

1. Read the first two words to your student and explain that most of these words are not real words. Tell the student you want to find out how well he knows the sounds that the letters stand for.
2. Have him read the entire first row across the top of the page without help. Tell him to say "I don't know" whenever necessary.
3. Circle each one that he misses, using another copy for recording.
4. This test is recommended for grade 2 or higher.

Test 3: The RAD Test—Rapid Assessment of Disablement

Directions for Group Administration

Note: This test is not a diagnostic test. Its purpose is to provide you with a means of quickly determining which children in a group may have a "specific language disability." The test is designed for second grade and up.

Part A: Visual-Kinesthetic Memory

Directions: Print the following words or letters at least 1½ inches high with heavy black felt pen on white cardboard about 3″ by 8″:

1. bad	6. hobby
2. your	7. eighty
3. top	8. minnow
4. nuts	9. whenever
5. JKBF	10. stumbles

Show each card one at a time in the order given. (Do not print the number on the card. Just say the number as you show it.) Expose the card for about 10 seconds while the students hold their pencils high over their heads.

After you have turned the card over, count five more seconds and say, "Write word number one." The children are then to write the word next to the number one on their sheet of paper. Give them about 15 seconds to write the word; then ask them to raise their pencils above their heads again.

Repeat this procedure for each of the 10 words. Do not show a word again after you have turned over the card.

Directions for Scoring RAD Test: To derive a score from this test, simply add the number of correct items in the 20-item test. Now compare the papers in the bottom third of the group with those in the top third. Truly disabled learners will usually stand out. This is not a precise assessment, but it gives you a way to determine quickly which children need closer observation.

Part B: Auditory Memory and Visual Discrimination

Directions: Have the following words and letters ready to read to the students:

11. quick	16. mommy
12. fyqt	17. thought
13. saw	18. surround
14. bdec	19. running
15. bubbles	20. everyone

Say each word or series of letters. Say each one twice. While you are saying each one, the students should have their paper turned over. After you have said a word or series of letters twice, count five seconds and say, "Turn over your paper and find the words or letters in row one. Draw a circle around the word or letters I just said."

Allow about 10 seconds for them to circle a word or series of letters. Then say, "Put your pencil down and turn over your paper. Listen for the next word or letters."

Repeat this procedure for each of the 10 words or series of letters. Do not say a word or series of letters more than twice.

Directions for Scoring RAD Test: To derive a score from this test, simply add the number of correct items in the 20-item test. Now compare the papers in the bottom third of the group with those in the top third. Disabled learners will usually stand out. This is not a precise assessment, but it gives you a way to determine quickly which children need closer observation.

Student Form for the RAD Test

Student's Name ____________________ Grade ______________

Teacher's Name ____________________ Date ______________

Part A:

1. ____________________ 6. ____________________
2. ____________________ 7. ____________________
3. ____________________ 8. ____________________
4. ____________________ 9. ____________________
5. ____________________ 10. ____________________

Part B:

11. puick	qnick	quick	pnick	kciuq
12. fypt	tqyf	ftyq	fyqt	tyqf
13. was	saw	sam	mas	zaw
14. dceb	dbce	bedc	peqc	bdec
15. buddles	dubbles	selbbub	bubbles	bnbbles
16. mommy	wowwy	ymmom	mymmo	mowwy
17. thought	tghuoht	thought	thuoght	thuohgt
18. snrronud	surround	dnuorrus	sunnourd	surruond
19. nurring	runners	running	gninnur	rurring
20. evyerone	oneevery	evenyoue	everyone	evenyone

APPENDIX C

Phonograms and Vowel Patterns

Essential Phonograms List: Phonograms with Ten or More Rhyming Words

The VC (Vowel-Consonant) Phonograms (26)

Short A:	ab, ad, ag, am, an, ap, at	(as in *cab* and *mad*)
Short E:	ed, en, et	(as in *bed* and *ten*)
Short 1:	id, ig, im, in, ip, it	(as in *lid* and *big*)
Short 0:	ob, od, og, op, ot	(as in *Bob* and *God*)
Short U:	ub, ug, um, un, ut	(as in *tub* and *rug*)
Example:	Phonogram *ab:* Rhyming words: *cab, dab, gab, jab, lab, tab, crab, drab, grab, cab, slab, stab*	

The VCC (Vowel-Consonant-Consonant) Phonograms (23)

Short A:	ack, amp, and, ang, ank, ash	(as in *sack* and *lamp*)
Short E:	ell, end, ent, est	(as in *bell* and *send*)
Short 1:	ick, ill, ing, ink, int	(as in *sick* and *pilo*
Short 0:	ock, ong	(as in *sock* and *long*)
Short U:	uck, uff, ump, ung, ush, unk	(as in *luck* and *buff*)
Example:	Phonogram *ack.* Rhyming words: *back, hack, Jack, lack, pack, rack, sack, tack, black, crack, flack, knack, quack, slack, stack, whack*	

The VCE (Vowel-Consonant-Final E) Phonograms (16)

Long A:	ace, ade, ake, ale, ame, ane, ate, ave	(as in *lace* and *save*)
Long E:	VCE is an uncommon way of spelling the long /e/ sound	
Long 1:	ice, ide, ime, ine, ive	(as in *mice* and *hive*)
Long 0:	oke, one, ope	(as in *poke* and *bone*)
Long U:	VCE is an uncommon way of spelling the long /u/ sound	
Example:	Phonogram *ace.* Rhyming words: *ace, face, lace, mace, pace, race, brace, grace, place, trace*	

(continued)

WC (Vowel-Vowel-Consonant) Phonograms (8)

Long A:	ail, ain . . . . (as in *pail* and *rain*)
Long E:	eak, eal, earn, eat, eed, eep. . . . . (as in *beak* and *peal*)
Long 1:	WC is an uncommon way of spelling the long /i/ sound
Long 0:	WC uncommon except with oa, as in *goat* (none with 1 0)
Long U:	Several . . . . .withlessthanten:cool, room, moon, loop, boot
Example:	Phonogram *ail.* Rhyming words: *ail, bail, fail, hail, jail, mail, nail, pail, rail, sail, tail, vail, wail, frail, quail*

Oddball Phonograms (14)

ay, all, ar, are, (dare), ark, aw, ear, ew, ight, ind (find), ow (low), ow (cow), ore, orn

Words for Teaching Vowel Patterns

	Short VC	Short VCC	Long VCE	Long VVC	Long CV
	in	ink	ape	eat	he
p	in	sink	cape	heat	she
	at	ill	ate	aid	go
c	at	pill	plate	paid	me
th	at	spill	note	mail	by
d	ot	blank	lake	soak	fly
c	up	dash	like	boat	try
ch	ip	bell	five	feet	no
	top	send	came	road	Hi
	not	lamp	rope	train	my
	bud	best	nine	green	be
	fun	sick	flame	jail	we
	bed	bang	time	beak	so
	sad	spring	poke	pain	pro
	spin	hint	bone	mean	sky
	pet	sock	kite	clean	spy

APPENDIX D

250 Patterned Books

Adams, Pam. *This Old Man*
Ahlberg, Janet and Allen. *Each Peach, Pear, Plum*
Alain. *One, Two, Three, Going to Sea*
Aliki. *Go Tell Aunt Rhody*
Hush Little Baby
My Five Senses
Asch, Frank. *Monkey Face*
Balian, Lorna. *The Animal*
Barohas, Sarah E. *I Was Walking Down the Road*
Barrett, Judi. *Animals Should Definitely Not Wear Clothing*
Barton, Byron. *Building a House*
Buzz, Buzz, Buzz
Baskin, Leonard. *Hosie's Alphabet*
Battaglia, Aurelius. *Old Mother Hubbard*
Baum, Arline and Joseph. *One Bright Monday Morning*
Bayer, J. A. *My Name Is Alice*
Baylor, Byrd. *Everybody Needs a Rock*
Becker, John. *Seven Little Rabbits*
Beckman, Kaj. *Lisa Cannot Sleep*
Bellah, Melanie. *A First Book of Sounds*
Bennett, David. *One Cow Moo Moo*
Berenstain, Stanley and Janice. *The B Book*
Bonne, Rose, and Alan Mills. *I Know an Old Lady*
Brand, Oscar. *When I First Came to This Land*
Brandenherg, Franz. *I Once Knew a Man*
Briggs, Raymond. *Jim and the Beanstock*
Brooke, Leslie. *Johnny Crow's Garden*
Brown, Marcia. *The Three Billy Goats Gruff*
Brown, Margaret Wise. *A Child's Good Night Book*
Do You Know What I'll Do?
Four Fur Feet
The Friendly Book
Goodnight Moon
Runaway Bunny

The Important Book
Where Have You Been?
Burningham, John. *Mr Gumpy's Outing*
Cameron, Polly. *I Can't, Said the Ant*
Campbell, Rod. *Dear Zoo*
Carle, Eric. *The Grouchy Ladybug*
The Mixed Up Chameleon
Polar Bear, Polar Bear, What Do You Hear?
The Very Busy Spider
The Very Hungry Caterpillar
The Very Quiet Cricket
Carter, D. *How Many Bugs in a Box*
Charlip, Remy. *Fortunately*
What Good Luck!
Cook, Bernadine. *The Little Fish That Got Away*
Dalton, Anne. *This Is the Way*
Degan, Bruce. *Jamberry*
de Regniers, Beatrice. *Catch a Little Fox*
The Day Everybody Cried
How Joe the Bear and Sam the Mouse Got Together
The Little Book
May I Bring a Friend?
Willy O'Dwyer Jumped in the Fire
Domanska, Janina. *If All the Seas Were One Sea*
Duff, Maggie. *Jonny and His Drum*
Rum Pum Pum
Dunrea, Oliver. *The Broody Hen*
Edens, Cooper. *Caretakers of Wonder*
Einsel, Walter. *Did You Ever See?*
Emberley, Barbara. *Drummer Hoff*
Simon's Song
Emberley, Barbara and Ed. *One Wide River to Cross*
Emberley, Ed. *Klippity, Klop*
Enderle, Judith Ross. *Six Creepy Sheep*
Ets, Marie Hall. *Elephant in a Well*
Play With Me
Flack, Marjorie. *Ask Mr. Bear*
Fox, Mem. *Hattie and the Fox*
Gaidone, Paul. *Hetty Penny*
The Little Red Hen
The Three Bears

The Three Billy Goats Gruff:
The Three Little Pigs
Gerstain, Mordecai. *Roll Over*
Ginsburg, Mirra. *The Chick and the Duckling*
Across the Stream
Goss, Janet, and Jerome Harste. *It Didn't Frighten Me*
Greenburg, Polly. *Oh Lord, I Wish I Was A Buzzard*
Gwynne, Fred. *The King Who Rained*
Hale, S. J. *Mary Had a Little Lamb*
Higgins, Don. *Papa's Going to Buy Me a Mockingbird*
Hill, Eric. *Where's Spot?*
Spot Goes to the Beach
Hoffman, Hilde. *The Green Grass Grows All Around*
Hutchins, Pat. *Good-Night Owl*
Rosie's Walk
The Doorbell Rang
Titch
Ipcar, Dahlov. *I Love My Anteater with an A*
Joose, Barbara. *Mama, Do You Love Me?*
Joslin, Sesyle. *What Do You Do, Dear?*
What Do You Say, Dear?
Joyce, Irma. *Never Talk to Strangers*
Kamen, Gloria. *"Paddle," said the Swan*
Katz, Bobbie. *Nothing but a Dog*
Keats, Ezra Jack. *Over in the Meadow*
Kellogg, Steven. *Can I Keep Him?*
The Mysterious Tadpole
Kent, Jack. *The Fat Cat*
Kessler, Eleanor and Leonard. *Is There a Horse in Your House?*
Kimmell, Eric. *The Old Woman and Her Pig*
The Greatest of All
Klein, Lenore. *Brave Daniel*
Kraus, Robert. *Good Night Little ABC*
Whose Mouse Are You?
Kraus, Ruth. *Bears*
The Carrot Seed
A Hole Is to Dig
Langstaff, John. *Frog Went A-Courtin'*
Gather My Gold Together: Four Songs for Four Seasons
Oh, A-Hunting We Will Go
Over in the Meadow

Laurence, Ester. *We're Off to Catch a Dragon*
Lexau, Joan. *Crocodile and Hen*
Lobel, Anita. *King Rooster, Queen Hen*
Lobel, Arnold. *A Tree Full of Pigs*
Mack, Stan. *10 Bears in My Bed*
Mars, W. T. *The Old Woman and Her Pig*
Martin, Bill. *Brown Bear, Brown Bear, What Do You See?*
Fire! Fire! Said Mrs. McGuire
Freedom Books
A Ghost Story
The Haunted House
Instant Readers
Little Owl Series
Monday, Monday, I Like Monday
Sounds of Language
Wise Owl Series
Young Owl Senes
Martin, Bill, and John Archambailt. *Chick Chicka Boom Boom.*
Mayer, Mercer. *If I Had…*
Just for You
What Do You Do with a Kangaroo
McGovern, Ann. *Too Much Noise*
McMillan, Bruce. *One Sun: A Book of Terse Verse*
McNalley, Darcie. *In a Cabin in a Wood*
McNaughton, Colin. *Who's That Banging on the Ceiling?*
Memling, Carl. *Riddles, Riddles from A to Z*
Ten Little Animals
Misumura, Kazue. *If I Were a Cricket*
Moffett, Martha. *A Flower Pot is Not a Hat*
Neitzle, Shirley. *The Dress I'll Wear to the Party*
Nodset, Joan. *Who Took the Farmers Hat?*
Numeroff, Laura Joffe. *If You Give a Mouse a Cookie* If You Give a Moose a Muffin
O'Neill, Mary. *Hailstones and Halibut Bones*
Patrick, Gloria. *A Bug in a Jug*
Peek, Merle. *Mary Wore Her Red Dress*
Peppe, Rodney. *The House That Jack Built*
Petersham, Maud and Miska. *The Rooster Crows.*
Pinkwater, Daniel. *The Big Orange Splot*
Polushkin, Maria. *Mother, Mother, I Want Another*
Preston, Edna Mitchell. *Where Did My Mother Go?*

Quackenbush, Robert. *Poems for Counting*
She'll Be Comin' Round the Mountain
Skip to My Lou
Raskin, Ellen. *Spectacles*
Rockwell, Anne. *Boats*
Rokoff, Sandra. *Here Is a Cat*
Rosen Michael. *We're Going on a Bear Hunt*
Rosetti, Christina. *What Is Pink?*
Rounds, Glen. *Old MacDonald Had a Farm*
Scheer, Julian, and Marvin Bileck. *Rain Makes Applesauce*
Upside Down Day
Schulz, Charles. *You're My Best Friend Because*
Sendak, Maurice. *Chicken Soup with Rice*
Where the Wild Things Are
Seuss, Dr. *Dr. Seuss's ABC*
Sharmat, Marjorie. *The Terrible Eater*
Shaw, Charles B. *It Looked Like Spilt Milk*
Shaw, Nancy. *Sheep in a Jeep*
Shulevitz, Uri. *One Monday Morning*
Skaar, Grace. *What Do the Animals Say?*
Sonneborn, Ruth, A. *Someone Is Eating the Sun*
Spicer, Peter. *The Fox Went Out on a Chilly Night*
Stover, JoAnn. *If Everybody Did*
Titheriington, Jean. *Pumpkin, Pumpkin*
Tolstoy, Alexci. *The Great Big Enormous Turnip*
Vaughan, Marcia. *Wombat Stew*
Viorst, Judith. *Alexander and the Terrible, Horrible...Day*
I Used to Be Rich Last Sunday
If I Were in Charge of the World
I'll Fix Anthony
Waber, Bernard. *Dear Hildegarde*
Walsh, Ellen Stoll. *Mouse's Paint*
Watson, Clyde. *Father Fox's Pennyrhymes*
Welber, Robert. *Goodbye, Hello*
West, Colin. *"Pardon?" Said the Giraffe*
Westcott, Nadine. *The Lady with the Alligator Purse*
Wildsmith, Brian. *Brian Wildsmith's ABC*
The Twelve Days of Christmas
What the Moon Saw
Williams, Barbara. *If He's My Brother*
Williams, Sue. *I Went Walking*

Winthrop, Elizabeth. *Shoes*
Withers, Carl. *A Rocket in my Pocket*
Wolkstein, Diane. *The Visit*
Wondriska, William. *All The Animals Were Angry*
Wood, Audrey. *King Bidgood's in the Bathtub*
The Napping House
Wood, Don and Audrey. *Quick as a Cricket*
Little Mouse, The Red Pipe Strawberry and the…Bear
Wright, H. R. *A Maker of Boxes*
Zaid, Berry. *Chicken Little*
Zemach, Harve. *The Judge*
Zemach, Margot. *Hush, Little Baby*
The Teeny Tiny Woman
Zolotow, Charlotte. *Do You Know What I'll Do?*

APPENDIX E

Games

Word Chase

Materials: Game board (see Figure 1): place markers such as plastic cars or buttons; one die. Home spaces should be four different colors (same four colors as markers). You may wish to write the sight words on strips about ¾" by 1½". Glue clear plastic holders on the game board and insert the strips. This allows you to change the sight words whenever you wish. (Or make a new game board from a file holder.)

Object of game: The first person to get from his home space all around the board and back to home space wins.

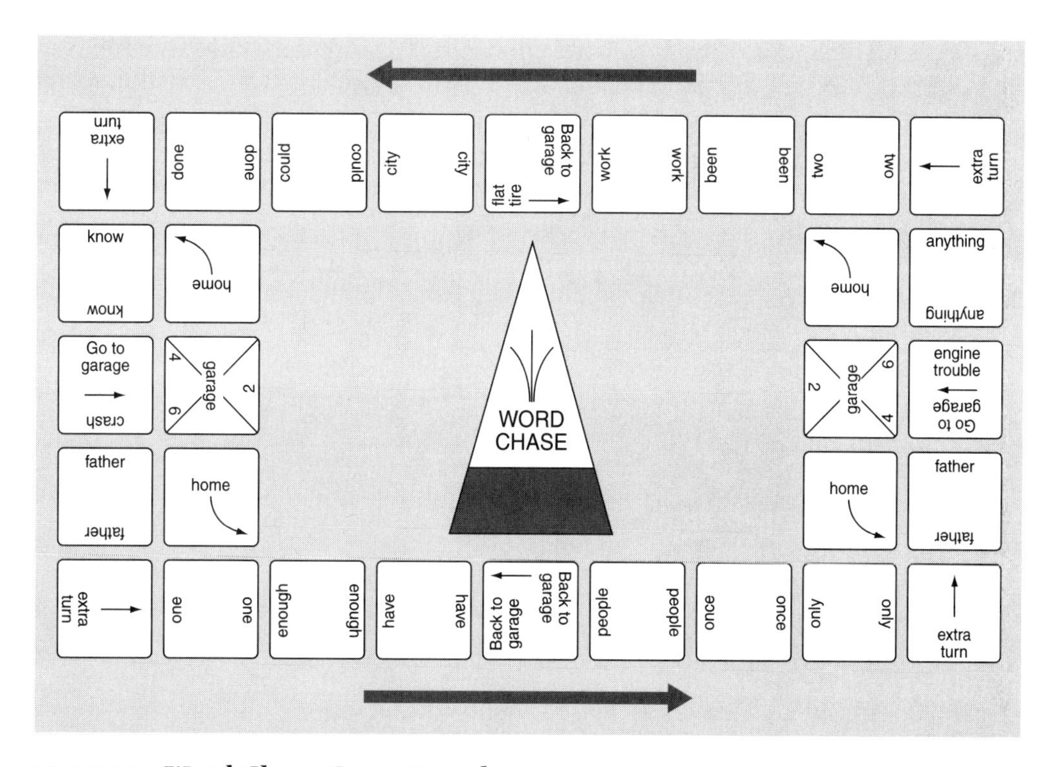

FIGURE 1 **Word Chase Game Board**

Procedures: (Two to four may play.)

1. Players roll die to see who goes first.
2. Each person rolls die and moves number of spaces indicated.
3. When a person lands on a space, he must read word out loud.
4. If a player doesn't read a word correctly (as decided by other players), he must move back to where he was.
5. The second person on same space bumps the first person's marker all the way back to home space.
6. After going all the way around, a player must roll the exact number on the die to get back into home space and win.
7. The player must roll a 2, 4, or 6 to get out of the garages.

Word Toss

Materials: Four boards, each about 1" by 6" by 30"; twelve 2" to 3" nails; three rubber or plastic rings (see Figure 2).

Procedures: (This game is best for two to four players.)

1. Each person tosses three rings. The person with the highest score goes first.
2. The leader shows a word with flashcard (about two seconds).
3. If a player reads word correctly, he gets to throw three rings.

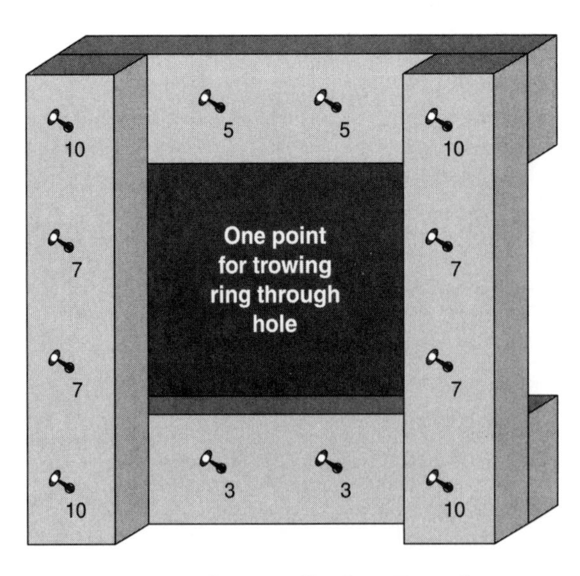

FIGURE 2 Word Toss Playing Board

4. The leader keeps score with tally marks.
5. Whoever has the most points at end of 10 minutes (or some other designated time) is the winner.

Steal the Words

Materials: 64* cards with 16 different high-frequency irregular words printed on them. Each word is printed twice on four different cards, once right-side up and once upside-down.

Object of game: The person with the biggest pile of cards at the end of the game wins.

Procedures: (Two to four may play.)

1. Draw a card to see who goes first. The person who draws the word with the most letters deals cards.
2. After shuffling cards, the dealer gives four cards face down to each person.
3. The dealer then places a row of four cards face up in middle of the playing area.

Wild Things

Procedures

1. Deal five cards to each player face down.
2. Place the rest of the deck face down in center of the table.
3. Turn the top card face up on the side of the deck to form discard pile.
4. The person to the left of the dealer begins play.

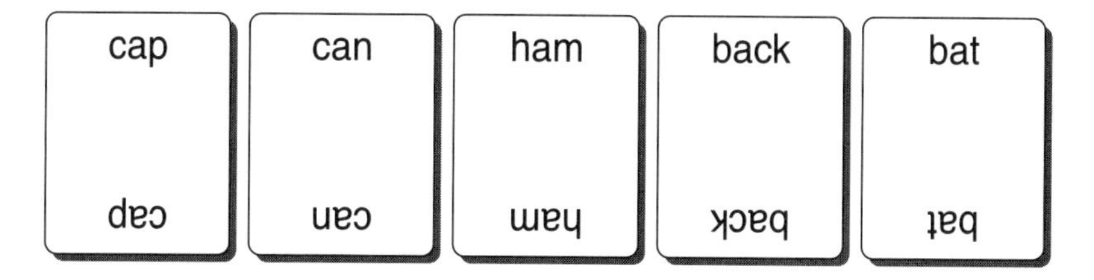

FIGURE 3 Phonograms as Wild Things Game Cards

*Business cards work well, especially if sprayed with plastic or hair spray after the words are printed. Check spray for running with one of the cards.

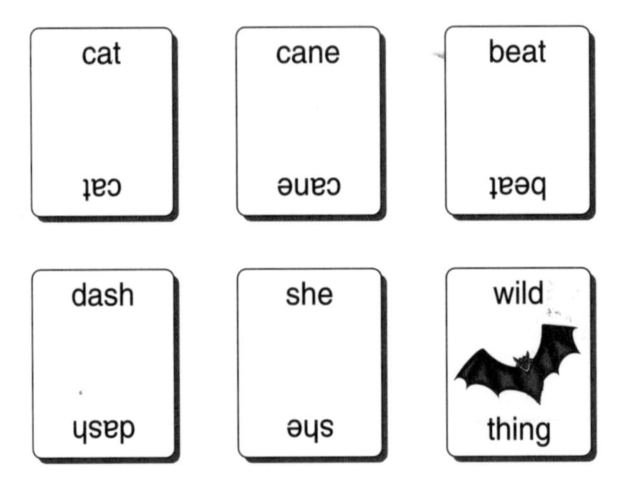

FIGURE 4 **Wild Things Game cards**

5. Each player plays (discards) or draws *only one card,* then it's the next person's turn.
6. To play, the player must be able to discard one card (VC, VCC, VVC, VCE, or CV). The player must read the pattern and word out loud to the approval of other players or lose turn. Example: If *hunt* is the top card on discard pile, a player must discard a VCC word like *mask* and say, "VCC, mask."
7. If a player does not have a word that follows suit, he may play a card having a word beginning with the same first letter as the top card on discard pile. This now changes the suit. Example: If *hunt* was down and the next player discarded *ham* the next player must play a VC word or another *h* word; he must also call out the pattern he has used and the word.
8. A player may change suit anytime by playing a wild card and calling out the suit he wishes to change to. Example: Plays wild card and says, "I want to change it to VCE words."
9. If a player does not have a playable card, he must draw *one* card from the deck and *lose a turn.* He may not play again until his next turn.

Value of game: Discriminating among five vowel patterns.

Adaptions of game: Use the five *r* patterns as suits: *ar, er, ir, ur,* and *or.* The player not only reads the word but calls out the pattern as well. Another adaptation is the use of phonograms as suits, such as *at, ack, an,* and *ap,* illustrated below.